A former veterinary science student, Victoria Heywood soon realised that her heart lay in dissecting human nature rather than animals. Since swapping surgical gloves for a laptop, Victoria has worked as a copywriter, journalist and author, both in Australia and overseas. She has written extensively on relationships, food and travel, and *Love Behind Bars* is her 23rd book of adult non-fiction.

Love Behind Bars

True Australian Stories

Victoria Heywood

The Five Mile Press

The Five Mile Press Pty Ltd
1 Centre Road, Scoresby
Victoria 3179 Australia
www.fivemile.com.au

Part of the Bonnier Publishing Group
www.bonnierpublishing.com

First published 2013

Printed in Australia at Griffin Press.
Only wood grown from sustainable regrowth forests is used
in the manufacture of paper found in this book.

Page design by Shaun Jury
Cover image © Shutterstock
Images on pp 227, 244 and 246 © Daniel Heiss
(www.danielheiss.net)

National Library of Australia Cataloguing-in-Publication entry
   Heywood, Victoria.
   Love behind bars : True Australian Stories / Victoria Heywood.
   9781743462966 (pbk.)
   Prisoners—Australia.
   Interpersonal relations.
   Love.
   Intimacy (Psychology)
   Prisons—Australia.
   Jails—Australia.
   Imprisonment—Australia.
   365.60994

Some of the names in this book have been changed.

For Jerome – stay on the right side of those bars, son.

Contents

Acknowledgements

ix

Prelude

1

Introduction

3

Chapter 1   **For Richer, for Poorer**: Jody and Richard

15

Chapter 2   **Love on Death Row**: Caitlyn and Timothy

39

Chapter 3   **Hell in Paradise**: Rachel and Perry

65

Chapter 4   **Prison Break**: Joe and Dawn

91

Chapter 5   **Lady Killers**: Women who fall for the baddest of boys

123

Chapter 6   **The Longest Stretch**: Gemma and Greg

145

Chapter 7   **Mind Games**: Frank and Amber

169

Chapter 8   **Blight**: David and Eve

185

Chapter 9   **Going Straight**: Chris and Brad

201

Chapter 10   **Love You a Legend**: Carolyn and Daniel

225

Acknowledgements

Many thanks to Greg Barns, Sharon J, Helen K, Sally N, the staff and interns of Queen's College, Melbourne, all the people I interviewed and the many others who helped me with the research for this book.

Prelude

I've had one speeding ticket in my life, a couple of parking fines and a warning against using my mobile phone in the car – and that was while parked on the side of the road. No-one from my family has ever been in jail, as far as I know, although my great-great-grandfather probably *should* have been in there from all accounts.

Mind you, I did learn to type in the Melbourne's Winlaton youth correctional centre (now closed). That early training has proved incredibly useful to me as an author, but I should perhaps confess that the only reason I was in there as a 14-year-old was that I'd had my appendix out and was not allowed to go to school. Instead, I went to work with my mother, as you do. Mum taught 'Winnie' girls for 20 years and was responsible for getting them back into the mainstream educational system on their release. (As a teenager, I was constantly warned that there was no point in going off the rails, as I'd only end up with my mother.)

So, in terms of the prison world, I'm practically a cleanskin. Some of the things I heard while researching this book gave me nightmares or made me cry, but the stories I heard also made me think more deeply about the cards some people are dealt – childhood experiences that shape a whole life; the far-reaching impact of one drunken error of judgment; the insidious impact of peer pressure; and how addiction is a disease that is perhaps not best treated by prison at all.

It also made me consider the question of love. How do you keep a relationship going when you know your partner is going to be in prison for the next 20 years? What kind of woman falls in love with and marries a convicted rapist and killer? Why would a mother leave her marriage, her children and her career to be with a violent career criminal? What is it like to be in love with someone in prison *with* you – perhaps another prisoner, or even a member of staff? What drives someone to pursue a relationship with a total stranger, and a convicted criminal at that?

Love does indeed work in mysterious ways. While some readers may find these stories heartwarming, confronting, tragic, romantic, perplexing or any combination, I'm in no doubt that these are indeed stories of love.

It astounds me that any of the prisoners and ex-prisoners I spoke to still had the capacity to fall in love after their life experiences, let alone sustain a relationship. The human desire to have an intimate, loving connection with another person can clearly overcome many things. I was also surprised by the fortitude and downright dogged determination of some of the women I met, who were hanging in there with partners despite financial and family pressures, distance, time, and even the possibility that they might never meet (as is the case of the Australian woman in this book who is in a long-term relationship with a man serving a life sentence in an American prison).

All the people I spoke to had very different stories, backgrounds and circumstances. The one thread that drew them together was their first-hand experience of love behind bars. For many, this book is the first time they've had the chance to tell the story of their personal lives, rather than the story of their crimes (or those of their partners). I thank them for their honesty, humour and time, and wish a better future for them all.

Victoria Heywood

Introduction

The voices of women are clearly heard in this book, but oddly enough, there isn't a single female prisoner or ex-prisoner among them. I thought it was odd that I hadn't been able to track down a single example until I spoke to Kerry Tucker, a former maximum-security prisoner and now a lecturer at Swinburne University, author, PhD candidate, regular public speaker – and board member of the Women's Correctional Services Advisory Committee.

While incarcerated, Kerry became the prison's lead peer educator, a role that involved liaising with, and advocating on behalf of, her fellow women in prison. All up, Kerry estimates she got to know 5000 women during her time inside. And she practically snorted when I asked her to help me find a woman whose relationship had survived the rigours of prison:

> Of the women I knew, almost every single relationship fell through while the woman was inside. And with recidivism rates currently at 73 per cent, I saw some of the same women time and time again over those five years, and not one of their relationships survived prison. Many times it was because the hubby said, 'Well, if the cat's away . . .' In some ways, I thank my lucky stars that my relationship had broken down *before* I went to prison; getting dumped in prison must be hell.

Kerry and her ex-husband are now on good terms: 'Maybe because he thinks I now know people who could get him killed!'

Kerry says there is another reason why a woman's relationship is likely to fail when she goes inside: '93 per cent of women in prison at any given time come from a relationship where there is domestic violence. Those violent men are not the type to stick around and support their partner.' In other words, guys who want a punching bag tend to want one who is close at hand, not one who is locked away and out of reach.

Kerry also says that no-one leaves prison as the person they were when they first arrived.

> Because the prison experience changes people in a fundamental way, there is every chance that the meek and mild girlfriend or wife who enters prison leaves it as a woman who has learnt to stand up for herself – strong, assertive and unlikely to take crap from anyone. Is it any wonder that their old relationship might not survive?

It is a very different experience for many men.

> When the woman is on the outside and the guy is in prison, their relationships seem to last better because women can be very, very loyal. I saw that over and over again; I still have many good friends who continue to love and support their husbands or boyfriends in prison.

Extreme Measures

Some women go to extreme lengths not just to support the man they love in prison, but also to get him out. Some people will be familiar with the case of the not-so-mild librarian Lucy Dudko, who in 1999 rented a helicopter on the pretext of wanting to check out the upcoming Olympic site in Sydney. Armed with a gun, she forced the pilot, Tim Joyce, to land at the Metropolitan Remand and Reception Centre where she picked up her lover, John Killick, who was serving 28 years for armed robbery. The helicopter took off to the sound of gunshots from the guards and cheers from the inmates. The pilot was released after he landed the chopper in a park, and the pair then hijacked a passing taxi. Dudko and Killick were finally arrested six weeks later. (Dudko was released on parole in 2006 after serving seven years of a 10-year sentence, but John Killick will not be eligible for parole until he is 71 years old.)

Less familiar, perhaps, is the tale of Fred Ward, more widely known as the bushranger, Captain Thunderbolt. According to popular myth, his Aboriginal wife, Mary Bugg, swam through the dangerous waters of Sydney Harbour – bolt-cutters clenched in her teeth – to help free her husband from the infamous labour prison on Cockatoo Island. While a number of PhDs, family histories and books debating the facts of the case have since been written, even the official website for Cockatoo Island prefers the romantic version:

Escape from Cockatoo Island was rare, not least because few prisoners could swim. Supposedly shark-infested waters around the island also tested the resolve of those bent on escape. But among the few who did, Frederick Ward managed it. In 1856, Fred Ward was sentenced to seven years on Cockatoo Island for stealing horses. In September 1863, Mary Bugg, his devoted part-Aboriginal wife, took the risk and swam to the island and left him the tools he needed to break free. Two nights later, Ward and his mate, Fred Britten, made a swim for it. Britten drowned, but Mary was right there on the shore waiting for Fred Ward, along with a fast, white steed, right beside where the Dawn Fraser Pool is now. Fred and Mary got away, and galloped off into the sunrise

What is known from first-hand accounts of the day is that the couple successfully eluded capture for almost a decade and managed to have a number of children along the way. Shockingly for those days, Mary Bugg was known to wear trousers and ride astride, and was noted for her raucous laugh and bawdy sense of humour. The couple clearly adored each other, at least according to Captain Thunderbolt's acquaintances, and I'll bet that if Bugg didn't actually engineer her husband's flight from Cockatoo Island, she was certainly delighted that he did escape. (Ward menaced northern New South Wales until he was shot by police at Uralla in 1870; Mary had reportedly died of pneumonia not long before.)

Dream Lovers

Whatever the facts behind Captain Thunderbolt's story, the romantic appeal of the 'bad boy' or 'the love that was meant to be' remains a very powerful driver for many prison relationships today, according to psychologist and author, Meredith Fuller. So while half the people interviewed in this book were in a relationship when they were sent to prison, the rest developed a relationship *while inside*.

It is surprisingly easy to meet someone of the opposite sex while doing time, say many of the prisoners from this book. Some had complete strangers writing to them, others fell in love with someone who came to visit, and one even had a relationship with his prison psychologist.

The motivation of the women is as diverse as the men they fall in love with, says Fuller.

Some women who end up with a complete stranger in prison have an aversion to commitment and intimacy, and may have difficulties sexually. They have the Mills & Boon romantic ideal of love, but great deficiencies or fears when it comes to being in a day-to-day relationship. Having a relationship with a prisoner gives them what they need – romance and attention, but little or no physical intimacy and no need to put up with the boredom or banality of everyday life.

There's also the added benefit that she has him where she wants him: he's unlikely to be seeing another woman or staying out late drinking with his mates.

A woman can feel very flattered by the attention of a prisoner. She becomes the centre of his world – the person he pours out his heart to in his letters and phone calls, the one he fantasises about. He has time on his hands to be attentive, to present himself in the best possible light, to write poetry, and to build great plans for the future, all without the pressures of having to hold down a job, pay the bills, put a meal on the table or otherwise function in society. Fuller puts it succinctly: 'He's not at home lying on the couch watching TV and yelling, "Where's my tea?"'.

Other women are more ambivalent about love than idealistic: 'They may be obsessed with their work or kids and not really want a full-on relationship, or they find that a regular romance doesn't suit them. It's a way of building a lifestyle that includes a degree of intimacy or pleasure or excitement without impinging too much'. For others, it comes from low self-esteem, believing that they are not good enough to have a normal relationship like other people, but can have one with a prisoner.

Do-gooders and redeemers are another case altogether. They feel an initial duty to help – maybe driven by religion or their profession – and then begin to believe that their love is the only thing that can save him. The power of that belief can be seductive, explains Fuller, but often these women can be quite naive.

They can be quite delusional. Yes, there are decent men who do bad things and bad men who do bad things, but there are also psychopaths, who will never change. Psychopaths often have charm too, which makes them doubly dangerous – when they turn that spotlight on you, it is very hard to resist. But psychopaths, in particular, cannot be fixed by the love of a good woman.

Take for example, the case of prison librarian Helen Cusack. A country girl, she was just 23 when she fell in love with inmate David Barac, who had kidnapped and stabbed his first wife in a jealous rage. She thought he had reformed and they were married after his release. Two months later, he stabbed her to death too.

'Excitement is another common driver – the "bad boy" syndrome, if you will', says Fuller. A lot of good, attractive, otherwise intelligent women fall for bad boys. It's similar to women who constantly fall in love with married men – they'd freak if he actually left his wife, or got out of prison in this case, and expected a real relationship. They need that thrill, or the possibility that something exciting or dangerous is going to happen. Take that element away, and the man becomes boring.

Falling in love with a largely absent man is also a trap for some women who have grown up with a distant or absent father figure – maybe he deserted the family, was emotionally distant, was a workaholic, or worked away from home.

For these women, being in a relationship with a man who is away in prison can feel familiar and somehow comforting. But it's not healthy. Sometimes it is a way of avoiding their own issues; the relationship is all about him and his case, and they don't have to confront their own lives, or grow up in a meaningful way. They are still trying to recreate the life they had as a child, as dysfunctional as it may have been.

Others simply love the spotlight, and they are the ones you'll find seeking out the baddest of boys and courting the attention of the press. 'In these cases, the women want to believe they are special, and they can only do that by having a connection with someone who is famous or notorious. They achieve status by association', explains Fuller.

And then there is old-fashioned love from out of the blue. Just like no-one can predict that standing next to a stranger at a train station might result in a happy long-term relationship, sometimes there is no pathology involved – just two strangers who happen to meet when one is behind bars, who fall in love, and live happily ever after.

Of Love, Loss and the Longer Term

Naturally, those who are already in a relationship have a different experience from the outset. Some partners are taken totally by surprise at the arrest of their loved one; others have perhaps seen their partner in court time and time again. Both, however, have a store of memories and a history of love as their bedrock when prison comes between them.

For the one who is imprisoned, grief is the overwhelming initial emotion, says Eve Barratt, CEO of Lifeline for South East Australia, and a specialist in suicide prevention within the prison system. 'During one of Lifeline's projects, inmates of the prison at Mount Gambier identified 37 losses that people experience when they enter jail – starting with the most obvious loss of freedom. And I'm sure we could have come up with even more losses if we'd had more time.'

For those who are already in a relationship when they enter prison, loss of that intimacy and love is a major cause of grief. 'And grief is not well catered for within the prison system . . . the results of that grieving process are often interpreted as behavioral problems', explains Barratt. Aggression and depression for starters, with suicide being the most final cry for help. And then there is the ongoing impact of prison.

> Most relationships are like a long-running play where each person knows the script and responds to the cues they are given by their partner. Prison changes all of that. Many criminals are insecure and suffer from anxiety, and the only way they can deal with it is to try and control either their environment or their partner. Going into prison where they have no control over what's happening to them or what their partner is doing can really eat away at them.

Barrett understands why some prisoners try to exercise some degree of control over the person they love, but she also knows that they are ultimately powerless. 'The inmate is absolutely reliant upon what the partner tells them is happening in the outside world. Some prisoners find that very difficult. Trust is a huge issue too. It's very difficult for men when the phone isn't answered: "Where is she? What is she doing?"'

On the flipside, prison can be strangely freeing for the partner on the outside, Barratt says.

> When someone goes into prison, there will be a very big shift in the balance of power within the relationship. If the power was evenly distributed, the impact is not so bad, but if the power was very much with the man, then the female will suddenly gain an enormous amount of power over everything from finances to how the children are raised. That can be a threat to any relationship.

Other, more practical, issues can make it difficult to sustain the relationship over the longer term too. The loss of one income and the resulting financial hardship can put the partner on the outside under considerable financial strain, perhaps even resulting in the loss of a home. There is also the strain of providing constant support. Kerry Tucker knows from her own experience that, as a prisoner, it is easy to think the world revolves around you:

> But life goes on for the family on the outside too. It's not always easy for the partner to look after all the practicalities and make regular visits, particularly when it involves a lot of travel or there are children involved; kids get caught up in sport and birthday parties and their own lives, and might not be enthusiastic about travelling for two or three hours on a weekend to visit prison and a mum or dad they barely remember.

As many of the people interviewed for this book point out, it's not just the prisoner who is under the control of the prison system. Transfers between prisons are common, and every time a prisoner moves, the partner and their family are affected too. Barratt describes it as a catch-22 situation. 'If the partner doesn't move as well, then they lose that regular contact. But if they do move to be closer, they may not have friends or family support in the new area.'

Out of loneliness, the partner outside may turn to dangerous coping strategies, such as alcohol or drugs or gambling that turn out to be problems of their own, says Barratt. 'In Mount Gambier, for example, every pub in town has gaming machines. For someone who is feeling marginalised or lonely, these places provide a very welcoming environment. And the long-term results of that momentary comfort can lead to further problems in the relationship.' Recently, residents of the small town collectively gambled away $18 million in a single year.

All women who decide to stand by their man, no matter what the hardships or where the journey may take them, have their own personal reasons. 'There is love, but for many there is also the feeling that they don't want to give up on everything they have built together. Essentially, they're saying: "I've invested so much of my life in this man, I have to keep going"', says Meredith Fuller. Some become experts in the legal details of their man's case. Some become fighters. Some become door mats or martyrs, doing everything that is asked of them and maintaining the traditional power balance of the relationship. Others simply muddle on, living on hope that things will work out in the end, and that love will triumph.

Genuine love and forgiveness *are* possible, no matter what the man might have done, says Fuller.

> In the scenario where two people love each other, the woman might say, 'I know this man. I accept the good parts of him, and I can also accept the bad parts. I love him, I understand what drove him to do the crime, so why would I cut out my heart and abandon him? I continue because I still love him and I have hope for our future together.'

This is not only true of those who are in a relationship at the time of the crime, of course, but also for women who meet their partner in prison. Fuller says that both are likely to employ one key coping mechanism: selective perception.

> If the man has been involved in something particularly nasty, the woman will often rationalise it. 'He was provoked, she was a slut, he was under the influence, or whatever . . .' She'll see his crime as an aberration that isn't really part of the man she loves. As a coping mechanism, she'll shut a door in her mind on all the bad parts, and only focus on the positives.

Love Beyond Bars

Eve Barratt says that if a couple have a strong relationship – built on trust, communication, respect, honesty and a sharing of power – then it is possible for love to survive in prison. But the long-awaited day of release can also bring its own challenges. The world will have moved on since the man went into prison, and this can be extremely testing, particularly for those who've spent years or decades inside. Some might never have seen automatic doors in action, used a mobile, sent an email, withdrawn money from an ATM or surfed the internet.

Long-term prisoners are also likely to suffer from crippling social anxiety, says Meredith Fuller, which puts an additional strain on their loved ones. 'Suddenly they're faced with a technicolour world that is right in their face. The bright lights, the people, the open spaces, the noise – it can be completely overwhelming.'

The important thing is to recognise that there will be a long road ahead.

> Partners and friends and family need to be patient, and understand what the ex-prisoner might be going through. As well as being pleased to be out, he could also be wary, frightened or angry, scared of the future and ashamed of his past. He'll be facing the judgment of society, while also probably struggling to find a new job and to re-establish his life.

They need to take it slowly, Fuller advises.

> It's like starting a relationship all over again so don't try to pretend that it's all going to be normal straight away. Take time to court each other, go out on dates, have time alone, discover each other anew, do things together that used to give you pleasure . . . simple pleasures such as walking together in the park can help you reconnect as a couple after all that time apart.

Both halves of the couple will be fumbling around in the new world order, perhaps renegotiating the balance of power and working out how to relate on an everyday basis again.

It can be a challenging time, so you both need to get as much support as you can. Sadly, government has slashed many psychological and relationship counselling services, making them difficult to access, but professional help early on can really help a couple stay on track. And there's no shame in admitting that you might need help.

In the end, it always comes down to the individuals, the dynamics of their relationship, and the love they have for each other. Each chapter of this book introduces a different couple who tell the story of their relationship. In all but a couple of cases, their names and some details have been changed to protect their identities as they focus on rebuilding their lives.

Chapter 1
For Richer, For Poorer

For Jody, life was great. Just 27, she'd been married for almost two years to 38-year-old Richard, and although he worked long hours as a loans officer at a major bank, she had her freelance artwork and her local sports club to keep her busy when he was at the office. Sure, they were only renting their house, but it was a comfortable three-bedroom place in one of Hobart's loveliest suburbs. The biggest things on Jody's horizon were the possibility of replacing their ageing car or perhaps taking an overseas holiday – something they had talked about for ages, but hadn't been able to afford. The last thing she expected, as Richard left for work early one morning, was for the police to arrest him in the driveway of their home. Soon she was to find out what exactly her husband had been up to.

'I'd had a problem with gambling since I was a teenager', says Richard. 'I started off playing illegal pokie machines; there were coffee shops with pinball and other machines, where they'd rigged them so you could play for real money if they knew you were OK.'

In those early days, finding illegal gaming houses was never a problem for Richard: 'How does the druggie recognise a drug dealer if they have never met before? How does a man find a prostitute? If you have a need, you will find a solution'. Richard's problem was specifically with pokies; buying lottery tickets or betting on the footy, the horses or the dogs never had the same appeal for him. Changes to the gaming laws only made access to pokies easier.

As a loans officer, Richard had been responsible for authorising loans for the bank's clients – mortgages, credit cards and car loans, whatever was needed. He established fraudulent loans for fictitious borrowers, with names either made up or plucked from the local telephone book. About 50 loan applications were made using this system. Richard had then transferred money from the loans into a bank account he'd set up under a false name. The fraud was discovered after a woman – who had a similar name to one of those taken from the telephone book as a loan applicant – complained to the bank after repeatedly being sent statements to a loan she had not applied for.

> Having that power was like a red rag to a bull for a compulsive gambler like me. I was like, 'Well I'll just organise a little $10,000 loan for myself'. One thing led to another, and by the time I was arrested, I'd taken about a million dollars all up. They had a list of all the loans I'd authorised, and I had to say which ones were for me and not real clients.

Richard is still surprised at how much money he'd actually managed to steal. And it wasn't as if he had been living the high life on the stolen funds.

> Finances in the family were always an issue. We kept our heads above water but only just, and only by robbing Peter to pay Paul. I was driving an old car that had done over 250,000 kilometres, we didn't do overseas holidays, and I'd never bought myself flash suits, worn a Rolex or bought Jody diamonds.

Practically every single cent from the bank had been fed straight into pokie machines, wherever and whenever Richard could find one.

> I'd go to work at 7.30 am, duck into the pokies afterwards and come home at 3 am the next day. Even in bed, I'd continue to dream about the machines, no matter if I'd spent 10 or 14 hours on them that day. Sometimes when I was having a good run, I'd still be there at 9 am from the night before, even though I was meant to be at work at 8.30 am. I've read studies in the US that have shown that gambling on pokies causes the same chemical reaction in the brain as heroin addiction. It can be that hard to beat. Another thing with compulsive gambling is that you live in a dream world. I kept thinking that I would have a big win and everything would be all right.

Financially, physically and emotionally, Richard's gambling problem had been taking its toll for some time. He could spend hours and hours sitting in front of the machines every day, not eating but possibly going through 60 cigarettes and numerous coffees in one session.

In his relationship with his new wife, he was also treading a fine line.

> I'd lie and make up all sorts of bullshit about why I wasn't home. And of course Jody loved me, so she wanted to believe me. I made up all sorts of excuses – a work trip, being in a car accident, even hitting a pedestrian one time . . . the stupid thing was that occasionally things really did happen to make me late home, but many times I'd just been lying. That's my biggest regret today – the selfishness of my actions and the way I treated Jody back then. She'd query where I'd been, and I'd somehow turn it around on her and make her feel guilty for asking a perfectly

valid question. Could I have been a bigger arsehole? Jody had no knowledge and no control at all, and the only reason she ended up in that situation was because she loved me.

The End of the Honeymoon

Richard is intelligent, articulate and clearly a very convincing liar. Jody was completely in the dark.

I had no idea that there was any sort of problem until the police came to the door that morning. The whole thing was absolutely surreal. I just couldn't make sense of the fact that there were people in our house, going through every room, every part of our life, and calling my husband a criminal. Trust me, it's not something you ever want to experience.

Richard and Jody were held separately while the police searched the house, so she was unable to even ask him what was going on. She was kept out the back in the kitchen. 'Before they took him away, they let him come and give me a hug but that was the only contact we were allowed. It was all so overwhelming. I remember actually sitting at the kitchen table, just shaking, and with no idea of what to do or feel or say.'

To this day, Richard feels guilty for what he put Jody through.

I'd never considered getting caught, or what might happen. Jody's world just collapsed around her. That's the thing about gambling – just like drugs or alcohol, gambling is a very selfish pursuit. You don't see the bigger picture and how your actions are affecting others. You become a brilliant bullshit artist so that people will believe the lies you tell them. You have to convince yourself that they are true too, because otherwise your world would fall apart.

Richard hadn't even been able to share the good times – his few, rare wins – with Jody.

> One day in particular, I got home and had $10,000 in $50 notes in my pocket. I knew I couldn't show Jody, because she'd realise that something was going on, but what the hell could I do? I could hardly put it in the bank! I couldn't even buy a new car or pay for a holiday, because then I'd have to explain where I got the money.

Before his arrest, Richard had thought about leaving his job – deluding himself that if the theft was discovered, they wouldn't be able to blame him if he no longer worked there. He'd even put in for leave and was planning to take a holiday and then never come back. He really thought he could get away with it – at least until the police cars blocked off his driveway that final morning.

Richard had been gambling solidly for almost 30 years when he was finally arrested. He had an earlier conviction for defrauding a previous employer, but had escaped a prison sentence. 'When I was arrested this time, I knew there was no way I could get out of it, so I put up my hand straight away and confessed to everything.'

Baptism by Fire

Richard was taken to the police station for further questioning about the million dollars that were missing from the bank, while Jody was left at home alone and in shock at how her morning – not to mention her life – was unravelling. But before Richard had been taken away, he'd been allowed to make a call to his sister, who lived just around the corner, and she had come straight around.

Amid the shock, the practicalities took over. What *do* you do when your husband has been arrested for embezzlement? Who do you call? What about his employer? What about clothes, toiletries, money, lawyers and other essentials? It was all very confronting for someone like Jody, who'd grown up in a good middle-class family and who'd never had any contact with the police or courts before. Richard's sister was equally bemused. She and Richard and their siblings came from a family of high achievers who'd never been in trouble. Jody and Richard's family suddenly found themselves on a very steep learning curve.

> I quickly found out that, for a start, I'd have to take Richard some clothes. There are no facilities for laundry or anything like that, so if someone [on remand] doesn't have anyone on the outside then they could be in the same clothes for weeks. Toiletries too. I had to pack up everything I could think of and take them into my husband in prison. It was horrendous.

The first time Jody saw Richard after his arrest it was from behind glass. 'It was just like a bad American film – you're in separate little cubicles, you pick up the phone and then you're talking to each other through two-inch-thick bulletproof glass.'

Jody doesn't know whether it was the shock of Richard's arrest or the environment in which they now found themselves, but she found it impossible to discuss anything personal or to talk of her anger and confusion and disappointment. 'Everything just shuts down and you just have to operate on a practical level – you know, what do we need to do next?'

Jody thinks that Richard was probably still in denial about his problem, his crime and its impact on their marriage when she first saw him in prison.

> It took a while for him to realise what he'd done, and the fact that it had been found out. The first time I saw him, he thought

that he could sort it all out – that he could fix it somehow. But embezzling a million dollars from your employer to fund a pokies addiction is not something you can easily fix.

Nor could Richard control his new environment. He describes his introduction to the prison system as both degrading and frightening. His first cell was lined with concrete slabs, and the only extras were a thin mattress covered in vinyl, a pillow and some bedding. He was relieved to find himself alone, but in the middle of the night a new cellmate arrived.

> He'd escaped from jail and then been captured. He had massive bruises where he'd been beaten up by the police, and for the next 24 hours he was coughing up blood and ranting about whom he was going to murder next. He clearly had serious mental and aggression problems, and I was locked alone in a cell with him.

Richard spent that first night fighting the pressing urge of stress diarrhoea, too scared to use the seatless, stainless-steel toilet for fear of upsetting his cellmate further. He passed a very uncomfortable night. The next morning, the cell was unlocked and he was let out into the yard shared between eight adjoining cells. The small space – about 20 by 50 feet – was now heaving with 30 other prisoners. There were two shared showers – the use of which was dictated by informal prison hierarchy. The same applied to the toilets. 'I saw some blokes going through their faeces in the toilet bowl to recover drugs they'd swallowed before being arrested, just so they could get their next hit. I'd never seen anything like that before.'

Once it became known what Richard was in for, some other prisoners caught the scent of money, if not blood.

They wanted to know where I'd stashed the money, but there was nothing left. I was broke. They just couldn't understand that I'd gone through a million dollars. They even indirectly threatened my wife, thinking that she must know where I had stashed it. I had to stand up for myself and try to make them understand that there really was no money left. The pokies had got it all.

Know Your Friends

You quickly learn who your real friends are when your husband goes to prison, says Jody wryly, particularly when your friends are unacquainted with the niceties of Australia's justice and penal system, except perhaps from the professional side.

There was a lot of gossip in our social circle, and some people tried to make Richard a scapegoat for other things that had been going on – discrepancies in the local sports-club books and stuff like that. Things that Richard had had nothing to do with. People kept on embroidering the story of what he'd done until it became completely ridiculous. I kept saying, 'that's not what happened', but no-one took any notice.

Jody trusted some friends who let her down very badly, including one who rang to offer support after seeing an article about Richard in the newspaper, and then gleefully shared Jody's confidences with their entire circle of friends.

I was at the point that if the Foxtel man had walked in the door, I would have told him everything. I have not spoken to that woman in all the years since.

Jody's family was shocked, protective and also very, very angry with their daughter's relatively new husband.

Let's just say, they didn't take it very well, but how *do* you take something like that well? Nowadays it is much better and they are fine with him. Most of the friends who got me through that time were people I hadn't been particularly friendly with beforehand. Some people I thought were really good friends didn't speak a word to me after it happened. It was all about how it affected them. And I'm sorry, it affected them *how*?

But some people surprisingly stepped up to the mark. Indeed, today Jody says that many of their main supporters were people they didn't know particularly well when it first happened.

A friend's husband – whom I didn't really know back then – dropped in very early in the morning not long after Richard's arrest to check that I was OK. He'd brought me a chart of the stages of grieving, and he said that although I hadn't experienced a death, these were the stages of grief that I was probably going to go through. I went to give him a hug and then just started crying and couldn't stop.

Jody describes the then relative stranger as someone who is a 'darling, darling man'. She still can't believe that after saying he couldn't stay long, somehow he ended up staying all day.

He'd arrived at 7.30 am, and a while later I realised that it was much lighter and I was still drinking tea and chatting to him. I looked at the clock, and it was 4 pm! Realising that I needed someone, he'd stayed with me the whole time without saying a word. Not once did I even notice him ringing work to say that he wouldn't be in. He was a godsend that day, and also afterwards.

There were some funny moments in between the rougher times. One friend used to call frequently in the early days after Richard's arrest, when the police still believed that Jody knew where the missing money might be.

> I could tell that the phone was being tapped, so we used to deliberately talk about the tea canister and the cistern and the washing machine – all the places that people traditionally hide money. The funny thing was that although these are the places they always search in movies, they'd never even lifted our mattress or looked in our cistern. It was like, 'You're going to go through my knickers drawer but you're not going to check the cistern of the toilet?' It was insane.

While Jody was discovering new sources of support and friends on the outside, she was also Richard's mainstay. His family had been both shocked and horrified by his arrest.

> The shame was the main thing for me. I came from a well-to-do, upper-middle-class family, I'd been educated at a good school so there was definitely an element of 'How the mighty have fallen'. One of my brothers happened to be close friends with a very senior policeman, so can you imagine how embarrassing it was for him to admit that I was now in prison. Another brother ran a successful business, and he had to change banks after 25 years because of what I had done and his connection with me. The whole thing was very distressing for all of them, and I'll live with that for the rest of my life.

Richard admits that being in prison shielded him from much of the fallout – that he wasn't the one having to worry about what might be in the paper and having to face the reactions of their friends and acquaintances.

The Abnormal Normal

Inside, Richard was finally getting the help he needed with his gambling. 'I did a lot of one-on-one counselling, and lots of gambling courses. I went to gambling support meetings inside too, and ended up becoming the jail coordinator and acting as a mentor to others.' Richard is proud of the fact that he didn't have a single bet during his time in prison. 'It's a big thing in there too; darts, pool, table tennis, cards – they'll bet on everything.'

Richard says that although in many ways prison is the worst thing that has ever happened in his life, in other ways it is the best.

It was inevitable though, looking back. I had to end up in there the way I was going. And at least it broke the spell of the pokies. The consequences of my actions before that were not sufficient to act as a deterrent. I would have kept on going if it hadn't been for prison.

Richard's pokies addiction introduced Jody to a whole new world too. She spoke to anyone she knew with personal experience of addiction, and then she reached out to the professionals.

They were as useless as you could possibly be. Their idea of support was to tell me that if I was feeling angry, I should go outside and throw some plates. I was like, 'And that will help me how?' They told me that I wouldn't feel so angry, but I pointed out that I also wouldn't have any plates!

Family support services at the prison were equally useless, mainly because Jody didn't fit the mould of the typical partner of a prisoner, or so she believes.

> They basically said that I must have known what Richard was up to and accused me of being in on the whole thing. Their attitude was, 'All the wives of the thieves we get in here are involved too'.' Jody describes their attitude as ghoulish. 'They just wanted to hear all the gory details from me – maybe it was to fill in their forms, but it felt like they just wanted a story to tell their friends that night. It was horrid.

Richard was sentenced to five years in prison for his crime, with three years of non-parole. As a result of his incarceration, Jody went from living in a comfortable three-bedroom house in a very comfortable suburb to a one-bedroom flat in a far less salubrious area. It was a very difficult time, to say the least, particularly as Richard had been the main breadwinner during their marriage. 'Suddenly I had to support him – to pay for all his needs, including his clothing, which changed every time he moved to a different prison. At one place it would be a green tracksuit with a white T-shirt; at the next, black and blue.'

The whole bizarre experience became Jody and Richard's normality. 'I'd visit, I'd come home, and then I'd count the days to the next visit. It became routine . . . it wasn't something I'd ever expected to do, but it became something we both just had to endure.'

Richard drew up a calendar on the first day of his sentence and crossed each day off, one at a time – all 1095 days of the sentence he was expected to serve before being eligible for parole. Jody couldn't bear the thought. 'If I'd counted all the days from the start, it would have been way too much to handle. I simply wouldn't have got through it.' Instead, she focused on putting one foot in front of the other, trusting that somehow things would improve. Looking back, there were times when she thought it was all too hard, but then she'd remember the marriage vows she'd made. 'Yep, that's what I promised I would do.'

When she made those marriage vows, little did Jody expect that it would involve a close encounter with another side of society. Prison visits were a particular eye-opener on a number of fronts. The never-ending procession of 'ferals' was a bit of a shock to Jody. 'Some women had seven children to different men and the kids didn't know whose father they were visiting.'

Jody didn't make any friends in the visiting room, despite seeing some of the same faces week after week. Inside, Richard took much the same approach – mainly because he was determined to just survive the three years and then leave it behind him. While some of the prison officers were 'psychopaths', others soon recognised that Richard was an intelligent bloke who just wanted to do his time and get out, and they treated him accordingly.

> They saw me as a guy who'd screwed up his life and didn't need them to screw it up more. And I was quite happy to do whatever I was asked to do – mop the floors or something. I didn't make any friends – you're never friends with anyone in jail, because you can never be sure what they want from you. I also didn't want anyone there to have any lasting association with me. I wanted to be an isolated unit, so that the experience would have the least impact on me.

Richard says that he is a very private person at the best of times, partly to do with the obsessive-compulsive disorder (OCD) that he now recognises he has always suffered from.

I've always had a thing for numbers and counting things. I can control it now, but at one point I could tell you how many steps there were from my front door to the post office, 800 metres away, or how many bricks there might be in a wall. I could also sit in front of a pokie machine for 10 minutes and tell you what percentage it was paying. It didn't matter what the odds were though; I'd always keep playing. At one time, I got to the point where I was dreaming in numbers and doing mathematical equations in my head, which did nothing for a good night's sleep or a chance for my brain to switch off. I was never fully rested.

Some of the characters he met in jail made a lasting impression, including one chap who seemed perfectly nice but who turned out to be doing multiple life sentences for contract killings.

The other guys warned me against him, saying that he was a nutcase and he might be nice to me now, but he could turn like that. Best to stay away. Another man called me into his cell and we had a lovely chat but it turned out that he was another killer and considered very dangerous.

With white-collar criminals, murderers, druggies and everyone else all thrown in together, there was no way of knowing who to trust or what to do.

You've got to be careful what you do or say, because of who you might offend. It can be little things like calling someone 'Champ'. That sounds like 'Tamp', which is short for 'Tamperer', meaning a paedophile. Calling someone a paedophile can get you killed. You don't whistle in jail either, because that's something you do to dogs. In prison, a dog is someone who snitches to the guards.

When you first go into prison, you're very naive and can do the wrong thing without even knowing it. Luckily, I was a reasonable size – 100 kilograms and six foot – so people thought I could protect myself.

Richard's worst night came when, for some unknown reason, he was briefly transferred to maximum security.

I had one night when I was in fear for my life. I'd been put into a triple cell and the other two guys were convinced that I was a police informer. I spent an entire night listening to them planning to kill me . . . they thought I was asleep and were discussing whether they could rip the leg off a table and beat me to death before the guards came in. All I could think of to do was to try and use my pillow to shield the blows . . . if they'd had a shiv [knife], I would have been stuffed.

In the event, his cellmates didn't make a move that night, but Richard had been so tense that he'd put his back out and couldn't walk. He was moved to the medical wing in the morning via wheelchair, and from there to another part of the prison. It was a very lucky escape, he reckons.

Richard spared Jody many of the details of his daily life at the time.

I always thought, 'Does she need to know this?' There was also an element of it being my punishment – that I had brought it upon myself, bucko, and that I should just shut up and suck it up. At the end of the day, I'd put myself in that position, so why should I burden her? What she had to go through was equally horrendous.

But for three years Jody was constantly worried. 'I couldn't do anything to help, and had no way of protecting him. And I knew that however badly the guards sometimes treated me, it must have been 10 times worse for him.' Jody, of course, had very personal experience of the guards, thanks to her regular visits to Richard. One particular incident is seared in her memory.

Before a visit, all visitors had to line up on dots on the floor about two metres apart. The sniffer dogs would go all over us and then we'd be patted down and scanned for drugs and other contraband. One day, one of the sniffer dogs knocked down a toddler, who immediately burst into tears. The mother was standing on a separate dot and wanted to go to her child, but the guards screamed at her to stay put. I mean, what was she going to do? The guards were the ones with the guns. All the visitors were treated like criminals – even the toddlers.

At that time, the couple was able to see each other three or four times a week, albeit through the bullet-proof glass. If they were lucky, they'd be the only couple in the room – if not, they might be surrounded by other prisoners, their partners and possibly children. Having a private conversation was only a dream on those days. However, they were allowed a one-hour contact visit every month. Then, Richard would be dressed in overalls fixed with cable ties so that he couldn't unzip them. 'But at least we could sit at a table and hold hands', Richard says.

His final months in prison were spent in a lower security facility. 'I was in a cottage with three other guys who'd all done over 10 years inside at that point. One was in for killing a cop, another one for killing his girlfriend, and another for slashing a guy's throat. And then there was me.'

Richard still can't quite believe that Jody stuck by him during this time.

> I wouldn't have blamed her at all if she had found the whole thing too hard. When we first met, I was a 30-year-old divorcee with a gambling problem; she was a 19-year-old country kid who'd grown up on the family farm and come to town for university. What happened next was not what she expected. It wasn't what I'd promised when she married me, nor what I would ever have wished for her. The fact that she stuck by me proves what a good choice I made!

The Afterlife

During Richard's time inside, neither he nor Jody had really planned what might happen on his release. Planning was too much pressure, Jody says. 'It was easier to say, "Let's just put it behind us, pick up and go on". I did make preparations for Richard to come home, but I honestly couldn't fathom how he would fit into my life at that time.'

Jody celebrated her 30th birthday just before Richard was released. It was a bittersweet occasion for many reasons – it was not how she'd ever expected to be celebrating, but then it was also a marker that Richard was on his way home. Having had three years by herself, in a new home where everything was done her way, Jody realised that she had to let go of the way she'd been living.

> I had to make a deliberate effort to let him be part of my new house and my life, which was difficult at first having been so independent for the last three years. I also had to make allowances for the habits he'd picked up inside – little things he had to do before he went to bed like checking that the doors and windows were locked, and that all the taps were turned off. Part of it was

about him feeling safe, but it was also part of the OCD that led to the gambling problem in the first place. It took a while before he stopped.

About six weeks before Richard was released, he was given day leave and then overnight leave, so he had a chance to reconnect with life on the outside. But when it came to the big day itself, he opted to make his own way home from prison.

Having anyone meet me would have felt too much like a celebration. I wanted to have time to reflect and get my mind together, to get used to the fact that for the first time in three years I wasn't being watched. That was a huge thing for me. Plus, going home under my own steam meant I was released a bit earlier so I could make the public transport connections I needed. I was let out before prison officially opened for the day – all the other guys were still locked in, which meant that I could go without having to see anyone.

Richard says that his time in prison still affects him.

Even now, ten years after getting out, I walk into the house and leave the front door open, and just lock the fly-screen. I can't bear being locked in anywhere. It's the freedom issue. I'd prefer not to be living on the ground floor too, so that there are fewer ways for people to get at me. Not a fortnight goes past without me dreaming about prison, and that's ten years after I got out. I still get vivid flashbacks and get very restless. The only thing that calms me is to be by the sea or to look at the sky. It was one thing having my body locked away, but when I couldn't see the sky, that's when I felt really in prison.

Social anxiety was another issue that still hasn't completely dissipated for either of them. 'When Richard walks into a group of people, he always wonders if people know about his past. We've learned to live with it over the years since his release, but it is always there.'

Richard admits that as a result of his prison experience, he's always looking for ulterior motives when people ask questions about his life, even innocent questions. 'I always wonder whether I can trust that person or not. It's not a nice way to live.'

Finding employment has been one of his biggest problems, particularly at the senior level he'd previously occupied.

> I can't apply for any job where they ask about a criminal record, and it seems that employers looking for senior staff generally want to do a probity check. If I ever do say that I have a criminal record, then that's it; I never hear back from them again. I'm yet to have one call-back from an application where I have admitted to my past.

Richard has even pursued jobs well below his experience level – in a call centre, for instance. 'I didn't even get an interview for that, and it's not like I am Jack the Ripper or something. But I never get the opportunity to explain – people just don't care.' He even came up with a brilliant fundraising idea for a charity, but when the organisers found out about his past, he was swiftly asked to cease his involvement. 'There was nothing in it for me – I was just trying to help raise money because I felt the need to give something back to the community, but they wouldn't listen. They even threatened legal action against me.'

Today, Richard is unemployed, which he admits does have its own stresses. He also worries about the lasting record of his conviction and imprisonment.

For three years, I disappeared off the radar of the Tax Office, Medicare, Centrelink, all because I was in the prison system. But every government department knows where I was . . . so if I go into hospital or something, it is there on my notes. I carry it with me everywhere I go.

Richard also has a huge restitution order issued by the court hanging over his head. The restitution order has no statute of limitations, so if by chance he does manage to get back on his feet financially and acquire assets – such as a house – then there is every chance that the state could swoop in and take possession of it.

The whole thing about doing the crime, doing the time, and then having the slate wiped clean is nonsense. I'm sorry, but in 20 years time I will still have it hanging over my head. Why would I risk buying a property if the bank could just move in and take it away? I'll never have a sense of stability again. Not only do I have the stigma of being an ex-prisoner and the difficulties involved in getting a job so I can rebuild my life, but if I do, then they can take it all away.

Coda

A few years after his release, Richard and Jody moved to the mainland. Most of their new friends have no idea of their past. Then again, they don't have their family and those friends who'd been supportive either. It's a catch-22, says Jody.

As for their relationship, re-establishing trust is an ongoing process. 'Whenever Richard is late home, there's always a little nagging doubt about where he has been. Sometimes I can go for months without thinking about it, but it's self-preservation on my part; once bitten, three or four times shy. I'm always a little on my guard now.'

Richard agrees, saying that he recognises that there will always be doubt, and he doesn't blame Jody for that. Rebuilding trust, both with Jody and their family and friends, is something that he knows can only be done slowly. 'I can't believe how lucky I am with Jody. I sometimes wonder if things would have been different if we'd been three years further down the line, when the gloss of the first years of marriage had worn off – not that there was a lot of gloss with my lifestyle!'

Richard took his prison sentence as a time to stop and reassess what was really important in his life. He came to the conclusion that he needed to celebrate and enjoy what he had.

> For 30 years, while I was gambling, I didn't appreciate my life. Gambling cost me all sorts of things – jobs, relationships, and sport. I had a chance to play one sport at the highest level, but it required too much commitment and too much time away from gambling. I look back, and think, what my life could have been like if it hadn't been for the pokies? From now on, I've vowed to live a different life.

And he knows he is lucky to still have Jody at his side.

> When you are together, you both change together. You either grow stronger together or you grow apart. But when you're separated by prison and only have a couple of hours once a week or a fortnight together, then you are both on different paths and changing in different ways. In the limited time you have together, it's difficult to convey how you are changing, so when you are reunited after three years, both of you are new people.

Richard is still in awe of the way Jody – a young woman who'd never really had to fend for herself – took responsibility for her life; a married woman but alone and also dealing with the stigma of a husband in jail.

> I wasn't party to all the changes that brought about in her. And she had no idea of how my time in prison fundamentally changed me. When we came back together again, it was like, 'Hang on, are we still the couple we used to be? Do we still have a relationship that we can pick up and carry on? That was the biggest question. Because we'd been changing independently of each other, we didn't know whether we would gel when we got back together.

Having a husband or partner go to prison is not something that Jody would wish on anyone. But she's proud of the fact that their marriage did survive. 'I've heard that if you can both survive the first two years of them being home, only then can you put it behind you.'

Recently, Jody and Richard celebrated their 15th wedding anniversary. The joke they have is whether they should include the three years Richard spent in prison. Is it really their 15th anniversary or their 12th? Or do they count those years inside as double? In that case it would be their 18th.

However you measure the time spent inside, Jody advises that you've just got to get through those years however you can.

> Laugh maniacally, write down nonsense – make it as surreal as you like because it is a surreal situation. One dear friend used to come over before each hearing, and we'd say, 'What are we going to do? I know, let's work out a smashing outfit to wear!' We always joked that we were going to write a book about what

to wear when your old feller is going to court. You have to have a sense of humour to get through something like this, otherwise you'll still be sitting crying at that kitchen table.

Chapter 2
Love on Death Row

Despair on Death Row

Despair etched into blank gray walls,
Filtered, muted light.
Every hour much the same,
As day melts into night.

Hopelessness evident in the eyes,
Of somber, solemn faces.
Knowing their life will end in these walls,
Knowing they'll die in this place.

Sadness escaping from the mouths,
Every time it's mail call.
Waiting for the letters that never come,
Trying not to let the tears fall.

Uncertainty clouding sleepless nights,
Thinking 'will I be here tomorrow?'
Wondering if there'll be any brightness,
To lighten this life of sorrow.

Confusion evident over the death penalty,
Is the punishment just or right?
Is it right to say an eye for an eye,
Is it correct to take a life for a life?

—CAITLYN, 24 JULY 2001

Should Caitlyn John's house in the leafy Perth suburbs ever catch on fire, there are three main things she plans on saving. First, her two kids – aged seven and three, the elder of whom has a severe learning disability. Second, her menagerie of rescued dogs and cats. And third, a plastic crate full of handwritten letters from her American boyfriend Timothy Ring – a convicted killer currently serving a life sentence for murdering a security guard during an armed robbery in Arizona.

Now in her late thirties, Caitlyn has always been a sucker for those in need of help – abandoned or ill-treated animals, lonely dogs looking for someone to exercise or play with them during the day while their owners are at work – and, over the last 12 years, prisoners on death row in the United States.

Caitlyn admits that her interest in death-row prisoners initially raised a few eyebrows among her close friends and family. After all, this was a woman who'd always believed in 'stringing them up'. Prison was too good for those who crossed the line and took another's life. 'I'd heard about women who fell in love with or married death-row prisoners and thought they were mad', she says.

What changed Caitlyn's mind was a trashy Hollywood movie about a prisoner who'd been wrongfully convicted and then executed. The film was based on a true story and, inspired and horrified in equal parts about the injustice done, Caitlyn and the friend with whom she'd watched the movie browsed the internet until they found the website for the Canadian Coalition Against the Death Penalty.

Part of the site was dedicated to convictions that had been overturned, others being questioned, and the ongoing fight to abolish the death penalty. But there was also a section where lonely American death-row prisoners could advertise for pen pals. It was kind of like an internet match-making site for some of America's most dangerous and desperate men – men who were facing the death penalty for the most heinous crimes, and who were reaching out for some kind of human contact – even if only through the occasional letter giving a glimpse of the outside world.

It certainly wasn't a case of life imitating art – or the comics. In the classic episode from *The Simpsons*, Selma had written to Sideshow Bob saying: 'Dear No. 24601, I need a man and cannot find one among the law abiding so am writing to you'. Caitlyn, on the other hand, was happily partnered and certainly not looking to complicate her life.

Finding love was the furthest thing from Caitlyn's mind. But as on a dating site, Caitlyn admits she looked for men who were about her own age – late twenties at that time – who perhaps shared similar interests or had a story that piqued her interest. Suddenly this former believer in the death penalty found herself writing to not one, but 14 different inmates across many different states.

The one rule she adhered to was 'no child killers'. Fortunately for Caitlyn, inmates in the prison system in the US have little privacy, and through Google she was able to track down details of most of their crimes. In many cases, she knew they were guilty, but she wrote anyway. For her, it wasn't to do with innocence, but with what made them tick. Caitlyn confesses to an abiding interest in psychology – what makes people do the things they do – and in another life would like to be an FBI profiler or criminal psychologist. Her letter writing was to introduce her to many men whose crimes could have filled a profiler's textbook.

There was Kia – a 32-year-old poor, almost illiterate, black man, who was 17 and out of his head on drugs when he shot and killed another youth during a robbery that netted him just $22.

There was Todd – who never talked about what he had done, but wrote in detail about life in prison and his despair. It was he who described his one hour a day in the exercise yard – surrounded by

15-foot-high brick walls with razor wire in a mesh over the top – as 'being like an ant at the bottom of a toilet paper roll'.

There was Granville, who was executed not long after Caitlyn started writing to him.

There was one religious fanatic who was determined to show Caitlyn 'the way, the truth and the light' that he had found inside. Being staunchly atheist, she politely insisted that he stop trying to convert her or their correspondence would have to stop. He didn't, so she swiftly culled him from her letter-writing list.

Another had too many pen pals so he dumped Caitlyn from *his* list.

There was the older man, an armed robber, whom she wrote to for a while but who died of a brain tumour before his execution date had been set.

One more pen pal was moved off death row in Illinois when the governor commuted all death sentences to life sentences. Doubtless relieved at his reprieve, the prisoner simply stopped writing to her.

There were others too. And then there was Timothy Ring.

Tim Ring had stood out from the other prisoners right from the start – mainly because his contact details included an email address, which seemed rather odd given that most prisoners in American prisons don't have access to the internet. Nonetheless, Caitlyn emailed him – a brief note describing who she was, what she did, a few brief details of her family and why she was interested in talking to him. It was nothing deep, and nothing too personal.

The reply came from Ring's father, Phil, who had put his son's details on the website in the hope that he might find some new friends on the outside, to alleviate the boredom of being locked alone in a tiny cell on death row for 23 hours a day – every day.

Phil would religiously print out any emails he received and then post them to his son. So far he'd had a couple of takers, so Caitlyn's email was just one of a few that he had received, but Ring was decidedly unhappy with his father for the whole hare-brained scheme. What kind of nutter would write to a death-row prisoner? Would they be religious freaks who just wanted to convert him? Phil warned Caitlyn that she might not ever hear back from Ring.

However, something about Caitlyn's initial email – perhaps her request that *he* not try to convert *her* – sparked Ring's interest, and the pair began to correspond. Initially, all letters went via Phil, then Caitlyn decided to write directly to Ring via the prison. It wasn't that the letters were particularly steamy – at least, not at that stage – but Caitlyn found it difficult to write details about her personal life knowing that Ring's father would also be reading her letters.

Somehow she wasn't so fussed about the prison guards, who she knew would be scanning letters just to make sure that no-one was plotting a breakout, or worse. She didn't really care if a warden in Arizona happened to know that she'd just adopted another dog, or that her kids had been on an excursion to the zoo. Or that she'd Googled Timothy Ring and was getting more and more intrigued by his case.

Soldier, Policeman, Bounty Hunter . . . Prisoner

Born on 29 October 1964, Timothy Ring had spent all of his adult life on the right side of the law, until his arrest. First, he was a military policeman, where he developed an interest in shooting. Then he was a policeman in New Hampshire and a confidential informant and bounty hunter – for the FBI, no less. He also, ironically, acted as a weapons instructor for correctional officers – the very people who were soon to be guarding him – and was a promising competitive shooter.

He'd been married twice – once to a woman who seemed only to want a sperm donor and who disappeared as soon as their child was born. He has no idea where she or his child are today, or whether they know what happened to him. His second marriage lasted rather longer, but came to a cold and abrupt end shortly after he was convicted of murder and sentenced to death. He received the packet of legal documents demanding a divorce, which he signed and returned; he never saw his wife or heard from her again.

The facts of the case – as outlined by the prosecution – were simple, and also shocking. It doesn't matter whether you believe, as Caitlyn does, that Ring had nothing to do with it, or whether you think he did. Either way, a man on a cigarette break ended up with a bullet through his skull.

On 28 November 1994, a Wells Fargo armoured van pulled up to the Dillard's department store at Arrowhead Mall in Glendale, Arizona. Courier Dave Moss left the van to pick up money inside the store. When he returned, the van and its driver, John Magoch, were gone.

Later that day, Maricopa County sheriff's deputies found the van – its doors locked and its engine running – in the car park of a church in Sun City. Inside the vehicle they found Magoch, slumped over on the passenger side of the van and dead from a single gunshot to the head. According to Wells Fargo records, more than $562,000 in cash and $271,000 in cheques were missing from the van.

A month later, tipped off by an informant, Glendale police talked to Judy Espinoza who believed that her boyfriend, James Greenham, may have been involved. He'd been behaving oddly and was suddenly flush with cash. The police started looking at Greenham and his buddy, Timothy Ring, as possible suspects.

The police investigation revealed that the two men had made several expensive cash purchases – two four-wheel drives and a motorbike – in December 1994 and early 1995. Espinoza also told them that Greenham had been away from home on the day and night of the robbery, and that he'd been very stressed all that week. After the robbery, he was much more relaxed and had given Espinoza and her mother a bag of coins and fistfuls of cash totaling over $1000 to pay some bills. And Greenham's friend, Tim Ring, owned a red truck – similar to the one that a witness had spotted near the scene of the robbery. Wiretaps were then placed on the telephones of Ring, Greenham and a third suspect, William Ferguson.

In one recorded phone conversation, Ring told Ferguson that Ring might 'cut off' Greenham because 'he is too much of a risk'. Greenham had indiscreetly flaunted a new truck in front of his ex-wife, who was pissed off at his display of sudden wealth. Ring said he could cut off his associate because he held 'both Greenham's and mine'. It's assumed he was talking about their shares of the proceeds.

The police engineered a local news broadcast about the robbery investigation, including several intentional inaccuracies in the report. On hearing the broadcast report, Ring left a message on Greenham's answering machine to 'remind me to talk to you tomorrow and tell you about what was on the news tonight. Very important, and also fairly good'.

After a detective left a note on Greenham's door asking him to call them back, Ring told Ferguson that he was puzzled by the attention the police were paying to Greenham. 'His house is clean', Ring said. 'Mine, on the other hand, contains a very large bag.'

On 14 February 1995, police staged a reenactment of the robbery on the local news bulletin, and again included a number of deliberate inaccuracies. On the police tapes, Ferguson told Ring that he laughed when he saw the broadcast, and Ring called it 'humorous'. Ferguson said he was 'not real worried at all now'; Ring, however, said he was 'slightly concerned' about the possibility that the police might eventually ask for hair samples.

Two days later, the police executed a search warrant at Ring's house. They discovered a homemade silencer attached to a Ruger® 10/22® rifle behind the hot-water heater in a corner of the garage, and a green duffel bag containing more than $271,000 in cash in a storage cabinet. They also found a note with the number $575,995 on it, followed by the word 'splits' and the letters F, Y and T. In their case against Ring, the prosecution asserted that F was for Ferguson, Y was 'Yoda' (Greenham's nickname), and T was Timothy. A search warrant served on Ferguson's residence also turned up $62,601 in cash. His share perhaps?

Testifying in his own defence, Ring said the money found at his house was start-up capital for a construction company he and Greenham were planning to form. Ring told the court that he made his share of the money as a confidential informant for the FBI and as a bail bondsman and gunsmith. But an FBI agent testified that Ring had been paid only $458, and other evidence showed that Ring had made no more than $8800 as a bail bondsman.

Ring's defence mainly rested on the fact that there was no evidence tying him to the shooting, and that he'd earned the money found in the garage through a series of confidential FBI assignments in Mexico – something the FBI denied.

So far, so slam dunk. But there was no evidence actually placing him at the scene of the crime, let alone pulling the trigger. It was Greenham's confession that put Timothy Ring in the hot seat for the actual murder.

Greenham explained that Magoch was a smoker, and while waiting for his partner to come back from the mall, Magoch had cracked open the door to have a cigarette, as the windows of the armoured van were not designed to open.

Drawing on Greenham's confession, prosecutors claimed that while Magoch was having his surreptitious cigarette, Ring picked him off with a single shot from about 40 yards away. The bullet passed through the door opening, hit Magoch in his left sideburn, exited through this right eyelid and then . . . disappeared.

Oddly enough, the bullet was never recovered. Nor was the cigarette that Magoch was supposedly smoking at the time of his death. And there was no blood splatter in the van from the killing shot. Magoch's spectacles, or what was left of them, also showed no traces of blood, despite the fact that the bullet had clearly exited from his eye.

Greenham claimed that after Ring shot Magoch, Greenham snuck over to the van, pushed Magoch over to the floor on the passenger side, got behind the wheel and drove to Sun City. There he met up with Ferguson and Ring, who unloaded the cash and cheques into Ring's red truck. As Greenham told investigators, Ring was cross that neither Greenham nor Ferguson had congratulated him on his shooting. It was a highly damaging bit of evidence that made Ring sound both callous and boastful.

On 6 December 1996, the jury found Timothy Stuart Ring guilty of first-degree murder, conspiracy to commit armed robbery, burglary and theft.

Greenham and Ferguson had pleaded guilty to second-degree murder. Greenham got 27-and-a-half years; Ferguson got 16 years.

Judge Gregory Martin of the Maricopa County Superior Court sentenced Ring to death. And it was Greenham's evidence that Ring had bragged about his shooting that decided the judge on the death penalty – for committing a crime in 'an especially heinous, cruel or depraved manner'.

A Question of Innocence

Jails are full of people who claim to be innocent, Caitlyn knows. But she believes that Tim Ring *is* telling the truth. Where did the bullet go? Why was there no blood splatter in the van, if Magoch had been killed there, as he sat in the driver's seat having a cigarette? How could the bullet go out his eyeball and not splatter his glasses with blood? Why was the cigarette never found?

'There is no way in hell that I believe he did what he was convicted of', says Caitlyn. 'The evidence simply doesn't add up.' Ring has told Caitlyn that he thinks that he was set up – possibly by Greenham, the guy who confessed and pinned the blame on him. But Greenham is in a different prison, and Ring has no way of asking him why he did it or what really happened.

Other press coverage from the day suggests that perhaps Magoch was in on the deal, and had been murdered later – outside the vehicle – to stop him talking. That theory would possibly explain the lack of blood splatter, the missing bullet and cigarette.

Whatever the facts of the case, all that is consuming Timothy Ring at the moment is getting out of prison. He doesn't even want to stay in America if he does get out. He's over the country and its justice system. He tells Caitlyn that if he gets pardoned, he's 'suing their arses off until their noses bleed'.

As Caitlyn sees it, if you are black, uneducated and poor in the US, it's easy to get railroaded. Ring was white and college educated, and still went down.

In one letter from Ring, early on in their correspondence, he'd posed a trigonometry puzzle for Caitlyn. Not knowing what it was about, she solved it and sent her answer back to him.

The puzzle had been Ring's reconstruction of the shooting. As he explained it, and as Caitlyn's mathematical workings showed, for him to have been standing where Greenham claimed, and to have been able to make the fatal shot, he would have needed to be 15 feet tall. It was enough to convince Caitlyn.

Early on, Caitlyn had worried about what to write to her pen pals, thinking that it would be cruel to torment them with details of her everyday life when they were stuck behind bars. But Ring explained that she was his one link to the outside world – that while he was stuck in a cell for 23 hours a day, her letters meant that he could experience the world through her eyes.

Caitlyn confessed that she'd once been in favour of the death penalty, but even that didn't upset Ring. He was impressed that she'd made the effort to find out more about the issue, and then had actually taken the step of writing. And had kept writing. And to 14 prisoners at that.

Today, Caitlyn continues to share her experience on many internet blogs and forums.

It's important to engage with people, to help them understand what these prisoners are going through. If I can convince someone else to write as well, or at least to consider the issue about whether it's right to kill people who've been found guilty but actually may be innocent, then I'd be happy. A lot of guys on death row don't get any mail, and don't have anyone to talk to. It's like torture. Their only human contact is with their guards. While most people on death row are not very nice people, it must be hard to think that no one cares about you. Not getting mail is like no one gives a shit if you're alive or dead.

As a result, Caitlyn always told Ring everything about her life. In a relationship at the time, she shared stories about her partner, the work she was doing with rescuing abandoned dogs, her extended family, her social life . . . it was a typical long-distance pen-pal friendship, but with one exception. Ring was still behind bars, and working hard on his legal appeal.

The letters were getting longer and longer. She'd include snippets from the newspapers, photos of her family and pets, pages of jokes printed from the internet, even a page with 'really stupid' old American laws. Likewise, Ring also sent her clippings from magazines or papers that he had enjoyed – a car that had caught his eye, a film or book review.

Sometimes the letters even overlapped, as often Ring fired off another one before he'd even had Caitlyn's reply to his last. Caitlyn was also a keen poet, and shared most of what she had written with Ring. Then she started writing poetry *for* him.

Ring had already told Caitlyn that she was the closest friend he'd ever had. Then a long handwritten letter arrived, telling her 'he hoped Caitlyn knew he was absolutely crazy about her'. Ring wrote that he recognised that he couldn't offer her anything, but that if he ever got out of prison, he wanted to be with her. Caitlyn wrote back immediately that she felt that he was the other half of her soul, and that if he was ever freed on appeal, she wanted him to come straight to Australia.

Caitlyn's family knew that she was writing to death-row prisoners. At first, Caitlyn's mother, Lesley, was horrified and worried that all of them were going to be murdered in their beds. Caitlyn couldn't help laughing. 'I explained that first they'd have to get off death row, then out of jail, and then across the sea to Australia. And *then* they'd have to find me! Also, why would they want to kill me when I've been writing to them, being nice to them and being their friend?'

While Caitlyn's initial interest had been to get inside the heads of people who'd killed, now she considers them to be friends.

Between Ring and Caitlyn, the letters began to flow even faster – 16 pages, 22 pages, a record-breaking 28 pages. 'It's almost like we share a psychic connection', Caitlyn explains. 'We like the same authors, the same music, think the same way about the same issues . . . we're both totally non-religious too, so there's no chance we're going to try to convert each other.' The only point of difference remains Ring's love of guns – and camping. Caitlyn doesn't do guns or camping.

By this time they were sharing intimate details – steamy letters would describe what they liked to do in bed, what they wanted to do to each other, what turned them off. And all the while, Caitlyn's partner, Jon, had no idea. He knew that Caitlyn had a number of pen pals whom she wrote to – but he didn't realise that things had become serious with Tim Ring.

Caitlyn and Jon had two children, but the strain of having less and less in common, not to mention a secret long-distance lover, was beginning to tell. The relationship ended and Caitlyn focused her attention on Ring. Then she heard that one of her original pen pals, Kia, had been given a date for his execution.

Kia was 33, and had been on death row for 16 years. He was a completely different person – he was clear of drugs, had spent his time behind bars improving his education and, by now, had become a close friend of Caitlyn. For Caitlyn, this was the hardest thing about writing to death-row prisoners – over the years of writing, she got to know these men well, but at the back of her mind she always knew that one day they would die. Knowing that Kia was about to die was devastating.

Anti-death-penalty campaigners swung into action. Even the victims' mother appealed to the governor of Texas asking for clemency. Caitlyn rang from Australia and spoke to the governor too, but to no avail. Kia was executed. It was the first experience Caitlyn had of a pen pal dying and it affected her badly for a long time. It also brought home to her, in the most painful way, that there was every chance that Ring, no longer a pen pal but a lover and confidante, would be executed by the American government too.

About five days after Kia's execution, a letter with familiar handwriting arrived. Caitlyn stared at it disbelievingly – Kia was dead. How could he be writing? But inside was a brief note, thanking Caitlyn for her friendship, explaining that he knew he'd made one dreadful mistake and that now he was finally going to pay for it with his life. Kia wished Caitlyn well, and that was that. By the time she was reading it, he was already dead.

Getting a letter from beyond the grave was devastating, and for a while Caitlyn couldn't bear to write to any of her pen pals, including Ring. 'The reason I didn't write was that the execution made it all too real for me. It scared the crap out of me – that these were friends of mine and the American government just decided to kill them.'

But then she thought of Ring – stuck in his cell for hours and days on end – waiting and hoping for a letter from her, probably wondering what had happened to her. She sat down at the computer again and began writing.

For a long time, she wrestled with whether she should tell Ring about Kia's execution or not. But just as she had told him about the release of another death-row prisoner – who'd been exonerated by new DNA evidence 14 years after being sentenced – she decided that she owed him the truth.

For his part, Ring likes hearing about others being released – it gives him hope. And while he had thought that perhaps Caitlyn had given up on him, and he had been angry that perhaps she'd just been stringing him along as a fantasy, not really caring about how he was feeling, he was just relieved that Caitlyn was back in his life. As for the chance that he would be executed, his legal team was working hard on a new appeal. They couldn't execute him while the appeal was working its way through the cogs and wheels of the justice system. He was still hopeful.

Inside Death Row

Hope is about the only thing that all death-row prisoners have in abundance. Hope and time . . . too much time, by all accounts.

In a cell just a few square metres wide, there is little room for possessions. Those with access to money, or connections, may have a television. Beyond that, there is room for a few books, some photographs, letters and paperwork. But not much room; Ring often has to discard books once he has read them, and old letters. Only Caityln's letters are a permanent fixture in his cell. Over the years, Ring had a couple of other people write to him too, but there was nothing like the connection with Caitlyn and he let the correspondence drift away.

Her letters are his lifeline, as he constantly tells Caitlyn. Ring, naturally enough, is in maximum security. There is no physical contact with other prisoners; he can talk with the other six prisoners on his block, but can't see them. The only time he is within touch or sight of another human is when prison staff escort him somewhere, or his lawyers visit.

In some ways, this puts Caitlyn's mind at ease.

I had a really bad dream one night that Tim was killed in jail by the other inmates, stabbed by one of them in the showers, and I woke up in tears. I emailed his dad straight away, and he rang the prison, but all was fine. I told Tim and he said that they didn't have any contact, let alone showers together, so there is no way it could happen.

At that time, Ring's biggest risk of death remained the state.

Ring has one hour a day in the exercise yard, and 15 minutes for showering. Often, he passes on the chance to go outside at all, describing the yard as even more depressing than his cell. 'I've asked him what it is really like', says Caitlyn, 'and he told me to go into the bathroom, take everything out, sit on the floor and imagine living like that 24 hours a day. I lasted 45 minutes. Tim does it for 23 hours at a stretch'.

Caitlyn reckons it would be like a living death – the loneliness, the boredom, being told when to eat, when to exercise, when to shower. And then there is the distinctive smell of prison.

Prison literally stinks, Ring tells Caitlyn, so these days she always sprays perfume on his letters. 'He says it is good to have something that smells good for a change. He tells me which perfumes he likes, and those he doesn't. It just gives him a little something extra to lighten up his day.'

Even while he was in the local lock-up for his court case, Ring was kept in isolation. Not just because he was an accused killer, but because of his work history as a policeman and in corrective services. He'd be a marked man should he be allowed in the general prison – police and wardens being generally despised by crooks for all the obvious reasons.

Ring's family continues to send him magazine subscriptions, so he's never without reading material. Caitlyn also sends Tim books occasionally – but it has to be via Amazon or another third party, as family and friends are forbidden from sending direct gifts, just in case they should try to slip some contraband between the pages.

Ring is not happy with Caitlyn spending money on him in this way, but is resigned to the fact that she does. And at least it's not cash. Caitlyn, at one stage, paid money into the commissary – where prisoners can buy items such as snacks and toiletries, stamps and paper – and Ring was incredibly angry with her. As he sees it, she needs to look after her family first. He doesn't want her spending her money on him.

Which is not to say that Ring doesn't also sneakily indulge Caitlyn when he can. Not long after they had fallen in love, Caitlyn was going through a rough patch in Perth. A family friend – a young boy – had committed suicide, and Caitlyn arrived back from the very distressing funeral to discover a note from the post office saying that there was a package waiting for her.

At the post office, the clerk handed over a massive box, about a metre square. Caitlyn wrestled it into her car, swearing that this was the last straw on such a horrible day. She ripped open the box without ceremony and inside was a huge queen-sized mink blanket, embroidered with a white tiger – her favourite animal. As it transpired, Ring's brother was with the military in Korea, and Ring had asked him to find something – a gift with a white tiger on it to send to Caitlyn – ideally something she could wrap around herself in his absence.

'It came on the most perfect day', says Caitlyn. 'If anyone had been watching, I must have looked like a total moron, but luckily there was no-one else at home. I just pulled the blanket out, wrapped it around me and sat on the floor sobbing for an hour.'

It just goes to show what kind of man he is, Caitlyn says: 'While he is basically fighting for his life, he still takes the time to arrange for someone to send me presents!'

The white-tiger blanket is likely to be the closest Caitlyn will get to holding Ring. She has never met him, never even spoken to him, and initially only knew what he looked like from mug shots in the press. Then Ring's father sent her a video tape – ironically, given his crime – of Ring demonstrating his prowess with a gun in a shooting competition. Caitlyn has played the tape over and over and over – just to see him and to hear his voice. 'I told him that he has the sexiest accent, but he claims that he doesn't have an accent – he says that I'm the one with the accent!'

Ring hasn't seen a video of Caitlyn yet, but she has managed to send him audio tapes – recordings of her dogs barking, her cats meowing, the kids mucking about and her being silly with a friend. Just ordinary stuff from home. Sometimes she writes a letter then reads it aloud on tape. One day she's hopeful that they'll be able to work out a way to talk by phone – perhaps by patching her in when he talks to his family, although she's not sure whether that would be allowed.

One Step at a Time

Today, Tim Ring is no longer on death row – he is re-sentenced instead to life in prison. Believe it or not, it is a step forward.

Google the name Timothy Ring or, better yet, *Ring v. Arizona*, and you'll soon see the uproar that was caused by Timothy Ring's appeal against his sentence. Not only did it see him escape the death penalty, but it also opened a new avenue of hope for possibly 800 other prisoners on death row across the country.

Capital punishment has long been a fiercely debated topic in the United States. Many question the fairness of the death penalty when evidence clearly points to severe racial disparities in how courts decide to sentence someone to death. The vast majority of those on death row are African American, Latino, Asian or Native American. And death sentences are imposed in disproportionate numbers when the victims are white.

Tim Ring is white and educated, and many of the oft-quoted statistics do not apply in his case. However, there has also long been vigorous debate about the way in which different courts across the country apply the death penalty. In the case of Timothy Ring, who was tried in Arizona, his life or death was in the hands of his judge at his initial trial.

Essentially, this is how the process worked in Arizona at the time. First of all, the jury decides whether the accused is guilty or not. Then there is a base sentence for the crime in question.

Take the case of a man who has been convicted of residential burglary at a trial. The standard sentence is five years in prison. But the criminal can receive a lighter sentence – as little as one year – or an aggravated sentence up to nine years, depending on whether the judge thinks there were mitigating circumstances or aggravating factors. (It's the difference between having a clean record and stealing to fund a daughter's hospital treatment, or being a habitual crook with a history of drug use and violence and more.)

At Timothy Ring's trial for murder, the jury deadlocked on premeditated murder, but found Ring guilty of felony murder – in other words, for the murder that occurred in the course of the armed robbery.

Yes, the jury decided whether the crime was committed 'beyond reasonable doubt' but in the days of Tim Ring's trial, the judge also had to record the aggravating and mitigating factors, and make his decision about sentencing on that basis.

Under Arizona law at that time, Ring could not be sentenced to death unless the judge found at least one aggravating circumstance and no mitigating circumstances sufficiently substantial to call for leniency. As the jury had convicted Ring of felony murder, not premeditated murder, Ring would be eligible for the death penalty only if the judge decided that he was the victim's killer.

At the sentencing hearing, the judge cited Greenham's confession and agreed Ring had been the, well, ringleader. He found Ring to be the actual killer, which meant that the death penalty was on the table.

In Ring's case, the judge decided that there were two aggravating circumstances that justified a death sentence. First, he decided that the crime had been committed for monetary gain, and second, that the murder was particularly nasty – in other words, 'especially heinous, cruel or depraved'. He did find one mitigating factor, too: Ring's squeaky clean record. Despite this, he ruled that there was no call for leniency.

Ring was, accordingly, sentenced to death.

After years of legal toing and froing, the appeal finally went to the Supreme Court and the much-anticipated decision, released on 24 June 2002, ended up invalidating Arizona's existing death penalty statute. In essence, the 7–2 ruling said that by allowing the judge, rather than the jury, to find the facts necessary for the imposition of the death penalty, the statute violated the defendant's constitutional right (under the 6th Amendment) to a trial by jury. Juries – not judges – should decide whether convicted criminals should live or die.

The ruling in *Ring v. Arizona* overturned the death-penalty laws in five states – Arizona, Idaho, Montana, Colorado and Nebraska – and called into question whether 168 death-row inmates in those states would be put to death. The ruling also had profound implications for many more hundreds of inmates on death row whose sentences had been determined by judges. (Nationwide, at that time, approximately 3700 people were awaiting execution for crimes committed in the 38 states that allowed the death penalty.)

Opponents of the death penalty were delighted. So too were Caitlyn and Ring.

Dream Lover

Whether on death row or imprisoned for life, in many ways Ring is the perfect lover, says Caitlyn. She has her own life and is free to do what she wants – to focus on her children, animals and family – all the while knowing that there is a man out there who adores her and constantly dreams of the day they will be together. She has one child with a severe learning disability, so life is pretty hectic in any case. Between frequent emergency visits to school to calm her son when he's disruptive, and her part-time work, there is little time for much else.

'Tim has told me not to put my life on hold, as it's unlikely he'll ever get out, but part of me can't help it', she says

Caitlyn doesn't actively discount the idea that she might find another lover – one who is not in long-distance lockdown – but says that if she did end up with a new partner and Ring was released, she would dump the other lover in a heartbeat to be with Ring.

'Tim isn't into kids at all, but says that because mine are part of me, he'd be happy to take them on – in a friend role if not as a traditional father.' Caitlyn describes Ring as a very blokey guy, but one who is very loving too. 'It's really rare to meet someone you're so in tune with. Every letter he writes is very romantic and is always signed "Love you always, Tim". He is absolutely the other half of me.'

Not that many of Caitlyn's friends know this. 'I'm open about the fact that I write to death-row prisoners – well, just Tim these days – but I don't tell people that we are in love. They would think that I am a nutter. People are judgmental about stuff like that. I should know; I was too once.'

Caitlyn's family is a different matter though, with both her mother and sister happily exchanging regular letters, and birthday and Christmas cards with Ring. 'Mum was panicked originally, but mums are mums and they will sometimes freak out for no reason. She's fine with it now she knows the kind of man he is. My nanna is probably another story. But other people don't need to know.'

Given the current divorce rate in Australia, perhaps there *is* something to be said for love behind bars. For a start, Caitlyn's relationship with Ring has lasted much longer than many marriages these days. And they still haven't run out of things to say, even when writing 20-page letters, which is par for the course for them. Caitlyn dreams of the day when they will be able to email each other and get instant replies, but doubts it will ever happen in Arizona.

'Getting the mail is always wonderful, but waiting for it is sooo hard. Often he'll send one letter, and I'll be in the middle of answering it, and another one arrives. We keep all our letters, and now we number them too. There have been a hell of a lot of letters over the years.'

As Caitlyn explains it: 'I can write anything to him. There is nothing he has told me that has put me off him; similarly, nothing I've said about myself has deterred him.'

From what she knows, she thinks that they're also likely to be highly compatible sexually. 'We do talk about it quite a lot. Things outside the norm that we're both attracted too – what we like, what we don't.'

Going without sex was hard for the first few years, Ring once told her. He also found it difficult having absolutely no contact with females – even just in passing – but that over the years it became easier. Then falling in love with Caitlyn brought back all the old feelings.

> We talk about everything to do with sex. He's said that the very first thing he would do when he got out is to go and get a full blood workup to get checked for all nasties. Only if he is clear, will he come over to Australia to see me. He's a really special guy.

Like most couples though, there's always the chance of a misunderstanding. The worst time for Caitlyn was when a couple of months went by without a letter from Ring. Initially thinking she may have said something to offend him, she re-read a copy of the last letter she'd sent him, but could see nothing there that could possibly be misconstrued. Tim's father had passed away by then, so there was no-one else she could talk to about what was happening.

Caitlyn spent hours searching on the internet to see if Ring had been executed at short notice, or possibly killed in prison in some other way. There was nothing in the news. Her letterbox remained empty too.

Eventually, Caitlyn found a forum for the partners and families of prisoners and asked if anyone knew what was happening in Arizona. She soon heard from someone else whose partner was in the same prison that the prison powers-that-be had put a stop to all mail – both in and out – as a general punishment. Even commissary privileges had been cancelled.

'It was my first introduction to some of the nasty stuff that prisoners have to go through', says Caitlyn.

It's like they are trying to drive prisoners insane as well as to punish them for what they have done. Can you imagine how it must feel to have no contact with the outside world at all? To wonder whether your wife or girlfriend or children are okay, or whether they have finally given up on you? It must drive the men nuts.

When Ring finally was allowed to write again, he wrote that he'd been really worried that Caitlyn might have thought that he was ignoring her. He'd been panic stricken not to be able to let her know what was going on. More than anything though, Caitlyn was relieved to hear from him and learn that no, she hadn't inadvertently said anything to annoy him.

Today, Caitlyn is pinning her hopes on the outcome of Ring's next legal battle. After getting off death row, his next herculean task is to overturn the original verdict and get a retrial. Should that fail, there is the risk that he may, in fact, end up back on death row again.

Caitlyn refuses to be daunted. 'I have to stay positive. It's horrible to think that I may never get to actually meet him.'

If he does get out, then there is a home here in Australia with Caitlyn. But they are unlikely to tell anyone how they met. 'Can you imagine what would happen if we told people that we met on a pen-pal site for prisoners on death row?'

Caitlyn wrote the following poem, about the fact that she could 'Promise You Nothing' in 2003, just as she began falling for Timothy Ring. As a way of trying to protect herself, she wrote: 'I can promise you nothing at the moment, except that I'll always be here at the end of a pen'. It has now been over a decade since they declared their love for each other, and Caitlyn is still hopeful that one day they will eventually meet.

⁂

Untouchable

I lay awake for hours last night,
My mind was filled with you.
I've thought about you since the day we met,
And I wonder, do you think of me too?
Do you ever wonder if this is all we'll have?
Only ever letters to sustain?
Am I fooling myself into believing you care?
Am I going to get hurt again?
Will there ever be a chance for us?
You can't answer that, I know.
You're untouchable at this present moment,
Through no fault of your own.
And there's no guarantee I'll ever touch you,
Or feel your skin against mine.
Your life is not in your own hands,
Fulfilment we may never find.
I told you once I promise you nothing,
And I wonder where that went?
I only know my feelings have deepened,
Through the letters that you've sent.
You're everything I've ever wanted in a man,
You're right in a way that I can't explain.
I know there are problems involved with you,
But I'm willing to risk the pain.

Love on Death Row

I don't know if we'll ever be together
I can't see the future ahead.
So at the moment, I guess I'm stuck,
With untouchable desire filling my head.

—CAITLYN, 24 DECEMBER 2003

Chapter 3
Hell in Paradise

Raised within view of Sydney Harbour and having been given every opportunity money could buy, Australian tourist Rachel Harris spent more than two years in prison with her boyfriend in Honduras – despite the fact that she had not been charged with any crime. Free to come and go, she chose to stay with the man she loved in a humid, stinking hell hole, crammed with humanity. It was a very, very long way from the comforts of middle-class Australia.

Rachel Harris hadn't been born with a silver spoon in her mouth, but she certainly landed on her feet when her grandmother, Claudette, left her the bulk of the family construction fortune when Rachel was just 16. Rachel's parents were given a much smaller number of shares and a life interest in the original family home – a sprawling harbourside house in Sydney's Double Bay.

Claudette had always been eccentric, and had never been particularly close with Louise, her only daughter, or Louise's husband, Richard. But the couple was still bitterly disappointed that Rachel inherited the bulk of Claudette's estate. The relationship between Rachel and her parents deteriorated rapidly, and while she managed to pass her final year of school, the tensions at home and the knowledge that she would probably never have to work for a living, meant that her results were less than stellar. She began a couple of courses of study, but nothing inspired her enough to really settle down. It was yet another reason for her parents to complain.

By the time she was 21, Rachel had gained control of her grandmother's estate and was independently wealthy. It had been a tough few years; now Rachel was ready for a break. With no money worries and no need to work, Rachel found that travel was just what she needed. What started out as a gap year, soon became two, then three, then more – with a few occasional jaunts back home to catch up with friends and do some short courses of study.

The world was full of young travellers, easily identifiable by their backpacks, their carefree attitudes and their boundless enthusiasm for new frontiers. Rachel felt at home among the nomads – drifting across Europe, across North America, then down to South America.

It was there, in the late 1980s, that Rachel first brushed against the darkness of the drug trade that, unseen and seemingly unstoppable, drives much of the economy of the continent.

> I was travelling with a friend and we'd passed through a little village in Peru and then a day later, we heard that it had been the scene of a massacre – 35 men, women and children had been killed. The drug bosses had literally just taken out the village in retaliation for refusing to help them produce cocaine. The woman who'd sold us cold drinks, the children playing on the street – all gone.

Before then, Rachel had experienced little of hard drugs and the devastation their trade can wreak – even on those who do not indulge. That was soon to change.

Finding Paradise

In the late 1980s, Honduras was well off the beaten path for most tourists. As the original 'banana republic', it's no surprise that bananas had long been the country's main export – making up as much as 80 per cent. Over the years, the spectacular economic success of the banana industry had made the banana companies extremely powerful, but there was also a flipside: bribery and corruption were endemic across the nation, from the highest levels of government right down to the man in the street who wanted to bend the rules to get a new building permit. Political unrest was everywhere, and anti-American sentiments were running high. Poverty was rife and many men carried guns and machetes for protection – and were not afraid to use them.

Although the social framework of the tiny nation was ugly, the environment was stunning – particularly the Bay Islands off the coast of the mainland, which were covered in pristine beaches, turquoise water, powdery white sand, and lush tropical vegetation. The reef system that rings the islands like a jewelled necklace is second in size only to Australia's Great Barrier Reef. Swarming with colourful tropical fish, the place has long been a mecca for divers and snorkellers, but when Rachel first arrived, there were relatively few Westerners there, despite the fact that it was only a few hours' flight from the United States. Even compared with the mainland, the islands had a mañana culture: businesses closed for siesta, posted schedules sometimes meant nothing, and there was not much to do but chill out and enjoy.

Rachel was in paradise. The locals were friendly, prices were cheap, and there was always a party going on somewhere. She made her home on Utila, the smallest of the major islands in the Bay Islands group at about 11 kilometres long and just four kilometres at its widest. Surrounded by the rich living reef, the island was crisscrossed by winding dirt roads leading to small villages and isolated bays. At that time it was also home to about 2500 people, most of whom were 'mextizo' which means mixed race – a mix of white, black and Amerindian. Few Europeans lived there permanently.

Like in Bali before the boom years, a symbiotic relationship had been established by locals and visitors. This was, after all, one of the poorest countries in South America, with two thirds of the population living in poverty. The tourists were welcomed as a source of income, and the locals, in turn, shared the secret delights of their island home. Also – perhaps inevitably – their beds.

'Lots of the island boys went out with tourist girls', said Rachel. 'But I stayed clear – at least initially. I was having too much fun just hanging out.' Rachel came to know one young island boy, Keith, and through him got to know his older brother, Perry. (English is widely spoken in Honduras, as well as Spanish, and many of the locals have traditional English names). 'I'd never seen Perry around before then because he never usually went near the tourists. He had a bit of a reputation as a Casanova, but only with the island girls, and already had one child that I knew of.'

However, Rachel was to prove the exception to Perry's 'no Westerners' rule. The pair began seeing each other, and about a year into the relationship, Rachel had drawn on her funds to purchase an airy local house – up on stilts to catch the breezes – and the two moved in together. This house was placed into Perry's name to avoid the red tape involved in a foreigner buying property – an obvious risk, but one that Rachel thought worth taking for her lover. They also bought a car and a couple of boats and set up a business, taking tourists on charters to go fishing, diving and snorkelling.

For a while it worked well. Rachel looked after the accounts and the administration, and Perry handled the front of house work, dealing with the tourists and running them around in the boats.

'I'm not an idiot – I knew what the islanders could be like when it came to a work ethic – so it was a bit of an experiment, but Perry did brilliantly', says Rachel. Their hard work was paying off, the business was ticking along nicely, and Rachel decided to take a return visit to Australia for a while, to catch up with friends. She wasn't worried about leaving the erstwhile Casanova on his own – they were in love, and he'd never really been interested in Western girls before her.

'I knew there was always the risk that he might sleep with someone else when I left the country on one of my regular trips back to Australia', said Rachel. 'And I always told him, "If anything happens when I am away, please tell me. I don't want to hear it from anyone else. I could probably forgive you for sleeping with someone else, even though I might bitch and moan and go out of my head a few times. But I would never, *ever* be able to forgive you for lying to me".'

But girls weren't to prove the initial problem. Just before Rachel was due to leave, Perry's brother Keith found a four kilogram bag of cocaine, well wrapped against the seawater, washed up on the shore. Now this might raise eyebrows in many places around the world, but in Honduras, not so much. It had probably been lost off a smuggler's boat. Rachel says:

> It wasn't uncommon – drug boats would throw stuff overboard and often it would end up in the mangroves. Drugs were getting worse and worse in the time I was there. Lots of the big guys on the island and on the mainland had made their money through big-scale trafficking. They might have later turned legit, but that's how they started out. It's not considered the same sort of crime as it is here.

Not that hard drugs were much in evidence on the island – some of the poorer islanders used crack, but for the rest, the usual drugs of choice were rum, tequila, beer and the occasional bit of marijuana. Perry wasn't a big drinker or smoker, and Rachel lived pretty cleanly too, preferring to spend her time diving, dancing and playing dominoes. By this time, she was well entrenched in the island community, as can be seen by a photo album that starts out filled with lots of white faces and ends up filled with photos of her black islander friends.

She'd never even touched cocaine herself – the memory of the Peruvian village massacre still loomed large in her mind. 'I'd never tried it; in fact, I had a real bee in my bonnet about it', she says. But four kilograms of cocaine represented a fortune, and she could tell that Perry was tempted to get involved with his brother.

'Don't you dare do anything with those drugs. If you have one thing to do with that stuff, you can kiss my arse good-bye', Rachel warned Perry. Trusting that Perry wouldn't risk his relationship with her, or his comfortable life, Rachel returned to Australia.

Welcome to Hell

The first inkling that all was not well was when Perry casually mentioned in one of their phone conversations that Keith had bought him a motorbike. 'I went off my head', Rachel admits. Perry reassured her that he had had nothing to do with the drugs since she left, and although she thought something was going on, she tried to believe that Perry would not be so stupid.

The next phone call came from Perry's father, Washington. Perry and one of his employees had been arrested and flung into jail. They'd been heading into town to buy petrol and the police claimed to have found a bag of cocaine in their car.

Rachel was urged not to return to Honduras anytime soon. The rumour mill had gone into overdrive about Perry. As an islander with two boats, a car, a house and a successful business, the local gossips concluded that he had 'obviously been selling drugs'. (The fact that Rachel had funded their home and business was either unknown or ignored.) The next rumour was that Rachel was the criminal mastermind and that she'd left him there to sell the drugs; should she return, she'd be arrested immediately.

Unsurprisingly, Rachel delayed her return until it was clear she was in no danger of being arrested. Meanwhile Perry had been thrown into prison – no charges, no bail, no legal representation. It was like being dropped onto another planet for a well-brought-up girl from Australia who expected justice and truth to prevail.

> I came at the whole problem from a completely Western point of view. But I know now that you can't go into a completely different culture with your Australian hat on and expect things to work. If I'd known then what I know now, I would have just given Washington $10,000 in a case, and told him to take it to the judge and just get Perry out of there. But I'd never been comfortable with the bribery culture.

Instead Rachel left it to Washington, who was male, Perry's dad and an islander. Rachel assumed that all these things would help him navigate the intricacies of the local justice system more successfully than she could. But Washington had no chance – despite being a local, he had always been on the right side of the law, and therefore had no idea what was really needed to get his son out.

Perry was initially imprisoned in the local lock-up on the island of Utila. It was small, hot, filthy and fetid, and for the fastidious islander, Rachel imagined it must have been hell. 'The room itself was only a few metres long and 20 people were crammed inside – standing room only, and just a piece of paper to shit on. It was disgusting and poor Perry was there for a month.'

Then – still without a trial or any firm accusations – he was moved to the mainland prison, a cinder-block construction literally on the beach at La Ceiba. Hundreds of men and women were crammed into this squalid construction, possibly 100 metres long and 70 metres wide. This was to be Perry and Rachel's home for the next two years.

Rachel's Return

Rachel had flown back to Honduras as a woman on a mission. Visiting Perry and the employee who'd been arrested alongside him, she heard their side of the story for the first time.

As they told her, they were in the car going into town to get petrol and the next thing they knew, the police had pulled them over and arrested them. They were driven to the lock-up and the car was confiscated. Most importantly, they swore there had been no drugs in the car – Perry had had nothing to do with them since his brother had found them on the beach.

Even today, Rachel remains convinced they were telling the truth about the drugs in the car. 'You know when two people are telling you what happened at the same time – they kind of flit around and interrupt, and talk over the top of each other. You can tell that it's the truth because even though they have different perspectives, the two stories essentially match. I had absolutely no doubts that what they told me was what really happened.' Rachel then read the police reports, and what she learned made her incandescent with rage.

One policeman said the arrest happened at a certain point on the road; another said somewhere else entirely. They couldn't even get the colour of the bag they supposedly found in the car straight. Again, one said it was blue – another one red, and a third one claimed it was green. The only thing the policemen did agree on was that they had found a bag in Perry's car and that it contained four kilograms of cocaine. I mean, can you imagine this happening in Australia – the police would be crucified by the defence. In Honduras, it's another world entirely. They didn't even bother getting their stories to match!

Rachel had never been angrier. Perry may well have known about the drugs, but she was certain that he hadn't been transporting them as the policemen were alleging. 'Months later we did a reenactment of what supposedly happened, and I have never hated anyone in my life like I hated those policemen. I kept looking at them thinking "You are lying fucking arseholes, and you know that *I* know you are lying".'

Today, Rachel is convinced that Perry and his employee were set up. Maybe Perry and his brother had annoyed someone and that person set them up with the police. Maybe the police themselves had heard the rumours of the drugs washing up, and decided to arrest them in the hopes of a pay-off. Either way, Rachel thinks they went after Perry rather than Keith as Perry clearly had more money, even if it was Rachel's money.

Still refusing to sink to the local custom of bribery, and firmly believing in Australian-style justice, Rachel prepared to fight for her lover's freedom.

In the Depths

Called Honduras by Christopher Columbus, who arrived there in 1502 during his fourth tour of exploration, the country's name literally means 'in the depths'. It's thought he was referring either to the deep waters off the northern coast, or to the country's landscape, which is characterised by continuous ridges of pine-covered mountains. For Rachel, 'in the depths' had an entirely different meaning.

The island of Utila was home to only a couple of thousand of people, and like in most small communities, gossip was rife. Rachel and Perry were the talk of the island, and while he was in prison on the mainland she had to face the curious stares and whispers every day. Rachel could have just visited Perry in prison, but she missed him and increasingly hated living on the island. To escape, she made a drastic decision: to go to jail herself.

This is where Honduras prisons differ markedly from Australian ones, Rachel explains. 'Visiting days were Saturdays and Thursdays – twice a week – and partners of prisoners were allowed to stay in the prison if they wanted. The only rule was that if you entered on the Saturday, you couldn't leave until the next Thursday, or vice versa.'

The prison itself was literally on the beach, with a floor made out of sand and thick walls of white cinder blocks reflecting the bright tropical sun. To enter, visitors passed through a barred entry section, then through another barred gate into the actual prison. Guards would search all visitors, but there was definitely some leniency, as many prisoners relied on food brought by their visitors to survive. Before rules became somewhat stricter, Rachel even used to smuggle in alcohol – she'd pour out most of a container of orange juice then top it up with rum. But Perry wasn't a big drinker in any case, so when liquids were banned from the prison, the loss of the occasional sundowner wasn't too much of a hardship.

Inside the prison itself, prisoners and visitors were subject to a strict pecking order, with the prisoners essentially running the prison and the guards just making sure no-one escaped. At the top of the heap was the President – a man called Marcus, elected by the law of tooth and claw from among the prisoners. He enjoyed all the privileges of the rank, including more spacious accommodation, and Perry was lucky enough to be allotted to his cell when he first arrived. It may have been because Perry had money behind him and could pay for a berth in the 'good cell', or because they were both from the island of Utila, but Rachel suspects that it was also because Perry had a natural, easy charm that often smoothed his way.

Others, less fortunate or with no money, ended up in the horror cells – huge dormitory cells where up to 50 people were crammed into bunks, stretching seven or eight levels high.

But even the 'luxury cell' was absolutely disgusting, says Rachel. With its tin roof and lack of windows, the tropical heat could be unbearable. So, too, could the smell. The only air to enter the room came through the door, and even that would be locked shut at night. But you got used to the smell, Rachel claims. 'You can get used to anything, even sharing a toilet with 21 other people.'

As this was the President's cell, bunks only reached three levels high. Perry and Rachel started out on the top – the worst level, where the air was thicker and hotter and ranker. 'As hot as Hades', as Rachel puts it.

> The bottom bunk was considered almost as bad, as you had two layers of people sleeping above you, or stepping over you in the middle of the night to reach the toilet. The middle bunk was definitely the prime position. At least you only had the chance of one person having to clamber down over you during the night or in the morning. And the air was much better too.

Facilities were limited to a toilet without a seat, and a bucket and tap for washing. This was shared between the 21 prisoners crammed into a space about the size of an average Australian kitchen. For privacy, there was a sheet stretched in front of the toilet; but there was nothing anyone could do about any sounds or smells. Rachel usually waited for the prisoners to leave the cell and head outside before she used either the shower or toilet.

And this was considered luxury compared with the other, less prestigious cells.

The two quickly settled into a routine – such as there was. From 6 am in the morning, the guards would begin unlocking the cell doors. Then the dreaded mariachi music would start up. Never a big fan, day after day of listening to mariachi blaring from someone's radio has put Rachel off for life. 'I hate it, hate it, hate it . . . but you wouldn't ever dare to tell them to turn it off.'

And you could forget about complaining about the food. 'The

prison didn't supply any', Rachel said. 'Prisoners with money could pay people to bring it in, and then pay other prisoners to cook for them. But the ones without money either went hungry or had to work inside the prison to get money for food. Nothing came from the authorities.'

Rachel used to stock up on food outside and lug it in when she returned to prison. There was also a shop selling basics like chips and cans of corn, for those who didn't have an outside source.

For cooking and eating, Rachel and Perry teamed up with a local, Ben, who'd been thrown in jail for having been found with a joint – yes, just the one joint – in his pocket. When Rachel met him, he'd already been inside for seven years.

'Ben had no-one to fight for him, and you had to have someone to fight for you or they just chucked you in there and left you to rot.' Rachel would buy the ingredients for the three of them and Ben would cook and share in the food. They'd also pay him a little bit of money so that he had cash to buy other essentials for himself.

Rachel explained that people didn't really talk much about what they'd been imprisoned for. It could be murder, it could be drugs, it could be violence, or it could simply be for annoying someone who was better connected and had the power to pull strings and ruin a life on a whim. Something like that happened a lot in a country like Honduras, as Rachel came to understand.

In reality, inside, no-one cared what you'd supposedly done. The Honduras system was so screwed that being in prison said nothing about whether you actually did it or not. Perry hadn't even had a trial at this stage, and there were many more like him – some who'd been in there for years without a trial.

It's worth noting that justice systems in Latin America differ greatly from those in Australia and much of the Western world, where defendants are presumed innocent until proven guilty and most cases go before juries. In many Latin American countries, on the other hand, the Napoleonic Code–based systems they use require defendants to prove they are not guilty if they are arrested.

The huge number of people in prison awaiting trial and a justice system clogged by delays are the two key reasons for the massive overcrowding that Rachel witnessed. Inmates can languish for months, or even years, as their cases slowly move through the backlogged judicial system. Even if innocent, people could be arrested, imprisoned and not have an actual trial for years.

At this stage, Rachel was spending five days a week in prison with Perry. She spent the other two back on the island where she would spend hours sitting outside the judge's office trying to get someone, anyone, to listen. Every so often, she'd see the policemen who'd arrested Perry drive past – in her and Perry's car, the very same car they had confiscated at the time of his arrest. It was adding insult to injury, and only after numerous complaints did the policemen stop using the car, leaving it locked outside at the police station (where it promptly rusted in the tropical damp).

When back on the island, Rachel generally tried to avoid the islanders and their whispers.

'In prison, you make friends where you find them. There was one American guy, Erik, who was in for paedophilia, and we became kind of friendly, being the only two Westerners in the jail', Rachel says, with a touch of embarrassment. 'Growing up, I never thought I'd be on talking terms with a paedophile.'

Rachel is also swift to point out that if she learnt anything in there, it was that just because people are accused of doing horrendous things, it doesn't make them horrendous people. 'I'm sure there are people who are bad through and through, but just because you murdered someone, that doesn't make you a murderer and nothing else. But if you have killed someone, it is basically how society will define you forever after. You are a murderer. Full stop.'

By this time she was also well aware of the flaws in the system, and that Erik's claim that he didn't know the age of the boy he slept with may well have been true. 'In the Honduran justice system, just because you may have been convicted of being a paedophile, doesn't mean squat.'

On the outside, prior to Perry's arrest, they had danced much of the time, and played dominoes when they were too tired to party or were recovering from partying. Inside was little different. 'We couldn't do much dancing in jail, but by God I played some dominoes', Rachel says.

Theirs was a relatively low-security prison and Rachel never felt directly threatened by the prisoners or their partners, many of whom also spent time in jail. 'You'd hear about the occasional stabbing or fight, but I never witnessed anything too bad.' She took care though, to stick to 'their' part of the jail – a risible notion, she now admits, as the whole place was only a few hundred metres square, albeit jam-packed with humanity.

Fortunately, Rachel was out of the jail, perhaps campaigning on Perry's behalf, during some of the worst of the guards' actions against the prisoners. 'On a day to day basis, basically they never entered jail. They'd just supervise from the outside to make sure no one was escaping.' Every so often though, the guards would want to make a point, and the prisoners would be dragged out onto the sandy soccer pitch at gunpoint, and made to lie there in the rain or blazing sun until the guards were satisfied.

Rachel's Australian finances and Perry's islander charm helped smooth the day-to-day obstacles for a while. But while living with the President was a step up from the hell-hole environment that others had to endure, it was with a sense of relief that Rachel and

Perry were finally allocated their own cell. How did they manage this? To try and alleviate the chronic overcrowding, the prison authorities had tacked on a few more cells, and Marcus the President looked after them yet again.

'Perry always got on well with people, and although he wasn't a big bloke, never had to put up with any shit from the other prisoners. Marcus and Perry had a healthy respect for each other and he really took care of us', said Rachel. After the rebuilding, Marcus got a cell of his own, and so did Rachel and Perry.

Their new cell was a definite step up – a single cell complete with double bed and, at last, a toilet and tap, bucket and dipper of their own. Everything they owned was kept in there: their clothes, books, domino set and a few posters. Rachel pinned up a few sarongs to cover the walls, and Perry managed to buy a stereo from another prisoner. There was even a TV set. Rachel had brought in a little stove too, upon which she would heat endless cans of Campbells' pea and ham soup. She hasn't touched it since.

Life was not too bad, aside from the fact that they were in prison, and Perry *still* hadn't had a trial. Despite the overcrowding – not to mention the lack of access to basic services such as adequate floor space, drinkable water, food and health care, and a lack of basic sanitary and hygienic standards – Rachel considers life in a Honduran prison somehow more civilised than in an Australian prison.

Partners could stay with their loved ones. They had some sense of autonomy and control over what they did and when. And they could create some semblance of a normal life – if they had money. But she also admits that it would all look rather different for those in a cell with 100 other men and no resources. And the prison they were in was the soft one – the other prison, tucked further up the hill, was another matter all together.

In the Eye of the Storm

In 1998, President Clinton famously stated: 'I did not have sexual relations with that woman, Miss Lewinsky'. The Queen Mother had her hip replaced, Google was founded, Posh and Becks became engaged, and the International Criminal Court was created.

Then, to put man's trivial concerns into perspective, came Hurricane Mitch. The most powerful hurricane of the 1998 season, it formed in the western Caribbean Sea on 22 October, and after drifting through extremely favorable conditions, rapidly strengthened to peak at Category 5 status, the highest possible rating on the hurricane scale.

At the time, Perry was still being held in the beachside prison in La Ceiba, and if not a holiday resort, it was certainly better than the 'prison up the hill'. That was where the biggest and baddest of the prisoners were held – judged not necessarily by the crimes they'd been accused of committing, but by whether they were likely to kill someone in prison or not. As a result, there were a lot of genuinely hard cases up the hill, and a lot of people who felt they had nothing to lose.

Hurricane Mitch had been hanging off the coast for a few days, and the Honduran prison officials were getting a little worried. Historic amounts of rainfall had been falling in Honduras, Guatemala and Nicaragua, and waves of up to 6.7 metres high were heading towards the coast. As conditions continued to worsen, it was decided that for safety – somewhat ironically – the relatively well-behaved beachside prisoners should be sent up the hill to join their (potentially) killer brethren.

As usual, Rachel was in prison with Perry as Hurricane Mitch approached. 'Of course, they didn't want to take us [partners] up the hill with the prisoners, so we were told to look after ourselves. We were literally booted out of the prison as the hurricane approached.'

'I thought, "Fuck, what am I going to do? I don't want to be in La Ceiba on my own in the middle of a hurricane".' Rachel went to the airport only to discover that all the airlines had moved their planes inland to one of the major towns. All except for the local airline, Rolands Air. 'And they were only still flying because they believed that God would protect them!' said Rachel. 'Come to think of it, they might have had something there. All their planes were second-hand and obsolete Aeroflot planes – even the Russians had decided that they were too old and rickety to fly – so they were pretty dodgy aircraft to start with! Imagine flying those planes through a hurricane.'

For once desperate to get out of La Ceiba and back home to Utila, Rachel took the last flight out of town on a Rolands plane.

It was the roughest flight I've ever had – the wind and rains were absolutely terrifying in such a small plane. A huge island woman and I were the only people on board and we just grabbed hold of each other across the aisle and clung together. She was praying the whole time; I just wanted to get home and I was totally scared.

When Rachel finally arrived back at her home, the friends who had been looking after the house were frantically attaching sheets of zinc across the windows in preparation for the full onslaught of Hurricane Mitch. They couldn't have been more surprised to see Rachel turn up in the teeth of the storm – particularly knowing how much Rachel hated flying at the best and most aviation-friendly of times.

Rachel and her friends saw out Hurricane Mitch from her home, and survived relatively unscathed. During it all, her immediate priority had been survival. But once the storm had passed, she was frantic to know what had happened to Perry and the other prisoners. The problem was that the hurricane had knocked out much of the essential infrastructure.

During Hurricane Mitch, waves 3.7 metres high had crashed relentlessly upon the coast and on the islands. But it was the rain that caused the most damage, peaking at nearly 910 millimetres in Choluteca, where nearly half a metre of rain fell in just one day – equal to over half a year's worth of the site's average annual rainfall. The Choluteca River flooded to six times its normal width, partially caused by Honduras's slash-and-burn approach to agriculture, which meant that the forests could not absorb any moisture. Meanwhile, up in the mountains, there were unconfirmed reports of up to 1.9 metres of rainfall, which flowed into the rivers and caused extensive flooding further downhill and widespread mudslides across the mountainous country.

Hurricane Mitch had caused such massive and widespread damage that Honduran President Carlos Roberto Flores later claimed that it had destroyed 50 years of progress in the country. An estimated 70 to 80 per cent of the transportation infrastructure of the entire country had been wiped out, including nearly all bridges and secondary roads; the damage was so great that existing maps were rendered obsolete. (About 25 small villages had been entirely destroyed by the landslides caused by the storm.)

The Aftermath

With the country in chaos and thousands dead or missing and presumed dead, no-one was concerned about the possible fate of one prisoner except for Rachel, and Perry's family.

After several days, Perry's aunt finally managed to get a phone connection, but the news from the mainland couldn't have been worse. There had been a fight at the prison and one man with a tattoo just like Perry's had been killed. Perry's father, Washington, came down to the Rachel's house to tell her that they thought it might be him. For three days, Rachel mourned Perry's death.

On day four Washington returned with the news that Perry was alive! A week later Rachel was able to beg her way onto one of the first flights to La Ceiba. Perry had survived, and had finally been brought back down to the beachside prison. Finally, Rachel was able to pass through the familiar gates to her prison home and hear Perry's story.

While she had been fleeing on the last plane to Utila, Perry and his companions from the beachside prison had been transported up the mountain to the hill prison. Sure, it offered safety from the rising sea, but for the anxious incoming prisoners, it was what waited inside that caused the real worry.

Unceremoniously, the beachside prisoners were dumped into the hill prison. The guards simply locked them into their new cells and departed. For Perry, and everyone else, it must have been terrifying. Not only was the hurricane now battering away at the flimsy tin roof, but they could also hear the sounds of the land literally slipping away around the building. Adding to the tension were the cries of the original hillside prisoners saying that there was not enough food and water to go around.

As Perry described it to Rachel:

We were all there trapped in our cells, thinking that the guards had locked us in here and left us to die. And then we heard that the hill guys were planning to kill the guys who'd come up from the beach. At the same time, all of us can hear the sounds of the landslides all around the prison. So everyone starts trying to break out of the cells, because we think that the whole prison is going to be buried. Even if that doesn't happen, *they* think we're going to eat all their food and drink all their water. *We* think they are going to kill us. And we all think that the guards have just left us here to die.

It was chaos. Many of the prisoners managed to break out from their individual cells. But far from having left them to their fate, the guards were still in their positions on the perimeter. Then the shooting began.

While Rachel spent her time protecting herself, her friends and home, and worrying whether Perry had survived the hurricane, Perry spent 'the whole fucking hurricane dodging bullets'. Rachel couldn't have been further away from the serene Sydney harbourside suburb in which she'd spent her formative years.

Rachel and Perry didn't know the tattooed prisoner who died during the hurricane. In all, another 11,000 people were also killed or missing presumed dead, and another 1.5 million left homeless, making Hurricane Mitch the second-deadliest Atlantic hurricane in history.

The damage had been done – worth over US$8.56 billion across the region. In Honduras alone, crop losses affected about a third of the country's arable land, with their staple domestic food crops of corn, sorghum, rice and beans all severely affected. The exports upon which the economy survived were also devastated: 85 per cent of their bananas were lost, 60 per cent of sugar cane, 29 per cent of melons, 28 per cent of African palms, and 18 per cent of coffee. Many villages were on the brink of starvation, while lack of sanitation led to outbreaks of malaria, dengue fever and cholera. Grim times, indeed.

Giving Up

Things weren't much better for Rachel and Perry. Rachel admitted, 'I'd already been though two years of living hell. And while I was glad that he survived the hurricane, I was at the absolute end of my tether.'

Their relationship was also deteriorating fast. Always determined and a resolute believer in justice, Rachel had almost worn herself out with the fight over Perry's innocence. She was getting thinner and more stressed by the day, the week, the month, and now by the year: 'I remember sitting on the steps at the airport, waiting for another flight back to Utila to petition the judge, and thinking, "What the fuck am I still doing here in this country?"'

As an Australian with knowledge of the Australian justice system, she had fought Australian style. 'I should never have tried it', she now admits. Back then, she was only prepared to admit to a few very close friends that perhaps if she knew he'd really done something wrong, she could leave Honduras with a clear conscience.

Perry, too, had changed over the time of his incarceration.

There are things worse than death and I think we both experienced them. Perry started going crazy after a while. At the end, he was not the man I'd been going out with – maybe not in the eyes of the guys in prison with him, but in mine. He was turning into a completely different person towards me. He was kind of pathetic, if I'm brutally honest.

Perry was relying more and more upon Rachel to bolster his spirits and get him out. But Rachel admits that she was getting weaker and less able to cope with the constant pressure. Always petite, she'd lost over 10 kilograms during her time in prison. Her comments to a friend about how much Perry had changed and how much she was struggling finally prompted the friend to speak up.

'You really have to be careful what you wish for', Rachel says.

I'd wished for an easy way out of the whole mess and then one of our best friends tells me that Perry had been cheating on me before the whole drugs thing blew up. When Claire heard that

Perry and I were fighting all the time, and that I hated the place and the people, she decided that she had to tell me.

In fact, Claire had made a few insinuations earlier on that Perry may not have been the paragon that Rachel believed him to be. 'I'd heard what she was saying, but I had shut her down completely. I didn't want to listen at that stage. I wasn't ready to hear it.'

Two and a half years down the track, Rachel was ready to finally listen. And hearing that Perry *had* slept with another woman – another Westerner on the island – was the last straw. Rachel wanted to hear it from the woman herself though, so Claire arranged a meeting between the two.

'It had happened during the month I was home, after Perry's brother had found the drugs in the mangroves. I suspect the affair would have finished the second I got back anyway, but Perry's arrest put a stop to it before that.'

Oddly enough, Rachel and her erstwhile rival got on famously, and Rachel still holds no grudge against her. 'She hadn't known that I existed, and although I'm sure she would have heard rumours of my existence, Perry would have reassured her that it was OK.' In fact, the girl had been mortified when Rachel returned to Utila and she'd seen Rachel go to war on Perry's behalf. 'I think she felt sorry for me, more than anything', Rachel says. 'She also suspected that Perry *had* had something to do with the drugs – the island had been awash in cocaine while I was back in Australia.'

Rachel went into prison one last time to confront Perry. Faced with Rachel's first-hand knowledge of his cheating, he had little to say. From the start of their relationship, Rachel had made it very clear that while she could probably accept him sleeping with someone else – if not like it – she would never accept being lied to. Whether he'd been involved in selling the drugs or not, she knew he had lied to her about the girl. It was with equal parts anger, regret and relief that Rachel walked out of the jail for the last time.

Perry was still awaiting a date for his trial, but it was finally time for her to give up the fight and leave Honduras.

Postscript

Several years later, Rachel returned to Honduras to finalise the paperwork and do some repairs in order to sell the home she and Perry had once shared and that had been rented out during Perry's incarceration. The house had always been in Perry's name; Rachel had always been aware that he could have conned her out of her investment, but somehow – despite everything else that had happened – she trusted he would do the right thing.

Now he was finally out. To this day, Rachel isn't quite sure what happened with his trial and how his eventual release came about, and she doesn't particularly care. 'All I cared about when I went back to Honduras was getting him to sign the papers so we could sell the house. I knew I would have to see him, but I had my emotions completely locked down.'

Waiting at the mainland airport for the flight to Utila, Rachel was struck by the physical memory of the many times she'd taken exactly the same route on her way back to the island from jail: the crushing sense of weariness, the tautness in her neck and shoulders. 'It was only at that moment I understood the price I'd paid for trying to support Perry. I couldn't believe I had lived with that tension for two and a half years.'

The island of Utila had changed dramatically from her time there. It was no longer a sleepy tropical hideaway. Development had seen many new bars and hotels spring up. In contrast, Perry seemed much the same, but all her old feelings for him had gone. 'I don't know whether he was ashamed or upset to see me. I didn't ask him any questions, and he never tried to justify himself to me.'

They spoke briefly about the house, then Rachel went out exploring the township with some of her old friends.

'Every bar we went into it, Perry turned up too. But we didn't speak again.' Perry left the island for the remainder of Rachel's stay there, only returning the day before she left to sign a final bit of paperwork. She hasn't heard from him since.

I accept now that I'll never know the truth of exactly what happened with the drugs. Who knows, if the policemen hadn't told such different stories about finding the drugs in his car, perhaps I would have thought more about whether he was innocent or not? Instead, there was me on my white charger, determined to save him at all costs.

As for his infidelity, his lies and the end of their relationship, Rachel thinks that Perry probably still has regrets.

He's not stupid. He would have known that I would probably forgive the cheating, but definitely not the lying. That was the real end of our relationship. I can see now that he was probably between a rock and a hard place – losing me meant that he was losing the one person who was actively fighting for him. I can see why he didn't want to tell me about the other woman. And how would I have reacted if I knew for sure that he had been involved in selling the drugs? It must have been eating him up inside the whole time.

Rachel doesn't hate Perry today, but thinking of what might have been still makes her sad.

He had so much potential, and in so many ways he wasn't like other islanders. He was capable and willing to work hard and smart, and good with people – a little guy who garnered respect from everyone he met. When I last saw him, he was sitting around doing nothing – he had a couple of kids that I heard of, but not much else happening in his life. It's a waste because he really could have gone far.

Chapter 4
Prison Break

Joe Tog's appointment to the position of caretaker on South Channel Fort in Victoria's Port Phillip Bay has to be one of the most unlikely recruitment decisions ever. From the résumés submitted, the field of keen applicants had been whittled down from 16 to eight and then to four before the face-to-face encounters with the bureaucrats.

'It can get pretty isolated out there, particularly when it's stormy', explained the government recruiters to Joe. 'You might go four or five days living on the island by yourself. How would you cope with that?'

Joe's response was direct. 'Have you heard of solitary confinement? I've done months and months of it at a stretch in Pentridge – oh, and a few other places in South Australia and Queensland, too. Five days would be a cinch.'

The man-made island housing South Channel Fort had been built in the boom days of the 1880s, when authorities in Victoria were convinced that the Russians would invade the colony and steal all its gold. About 100 soldiers were stationed there, and the tiny outcrop bristled with cannons, machine guns and a thorny hedge – planted as a last line of defence should gold-hungry Russians or other attackers decide to land. Sight lines in the thick walls allowed soldiers to track ships making their way up the channel past Blairgowrie and Rye. Should an attack seem imminent, the soldiers could detonate mines buried in the sand below. But such a crisis never arose.

The new caretaker was going to be the first person to live on the island since the soldiers left at around the turn of the 20th century when they realised that the Russians didn't look like they were going to raid Melbourne for its gold any time soon. Since then, the island had only been used for storing mundane explosives for dredging. Then, in the 1980s, the Victorian Tourism Commission took over the derelict island and opened it to the public. Now they wanted a caretaker to live on the isolated spot to ensure it wasn't going to be vandalised by hooligans – hooligans with access to a boat, that is, given that the island was offshore and only accessible by sea.

The next curly question in the job interview was about Joe's resourcefulness. 'I asked them how they defined "resourceful" and they wanted to know how I'd cope if I had to make do with very little, such as would be the case if the weather turned bad and I was stuck on the island, or if I had to confront some vandals.'

Again Joe was upfront about his past. 'I asked them whether escaping from prison a number of times counted, and whether managing to stay on the run for months at a time was sufficient to prove my "resourcefulness".'

As for confronting people who wanted to stir up a bit of trouble, Joe had received a very useful education in defusing tricky situations, both on the outside and during his stints in prison where he was locked up with some of Australia's most notorious crooks. He was stocky, well muscled, covered in prison tattoos and, despite his twinkly visage, would doubtless scare the pants off any boating yobbo foolish enough to try something. Who knows what examples of resourcefulness the other applicants came up with, but the job was soon Joe's.

It was a classic case of poacher turned gamekeeper. Here was a bloke who was not only used to living in solitude behind foot-thick stone walls, but one who had already proved that he could survive in some of the toughest environments around – and could live off meager resources and the faintest whiff of hope when circumstances dictated it necessary.

For Joe to get the role of caretaker on this remote island – just off the coast of Sorrento – was a triumph for a man who'd left school at 13, been the youngest ever prisoner to be sent to Pentridge, received most of his education from older crooks, and whose CV would raise eyebrows among even the most liberal of employers.

This was a man who had served time in H-Division Pentridge, S-division Yatala Prison, and the Cages in Boggo Road; a man who had escaped numerous times, been shot in the head twice, stabbed in a prison-yard dispute and taken part in a number of prison riots.

Who would have thought that the Victorian government itself would one day employ the same man who had been featured on the Australia's Most Wanted List throughout most of the 1970s and 1980s? If it was a triumph of bureaucratic imagination over bureaucratic fear of the 'other', the act of employing Joe Tog was also to prove his lifeline.

'When I was released from prison the last time, I was sent off to VACRO [the Victorian Association for the Care and Resettlement of Offenders]. I would never, never, ever have got that job without their help, as I couldn't see that there was any value in the skills I had. I had no idea that some of the skills I'd developed over the years as a safe-breaker would be transferrable to the everyday world.'

Joe's caseworkers proved themselves to be 'bloody brilliant'. So what if Joe had previously had a career as a safe-breaker? Didn't that also mean that he was good at welding and knew his way around many of the tools used in other, rather less criminal, endeavours? As for more nebulous skills such as organisation, planning, strategic thinking and project implementation – the fact that he'd survived so long on the run and committed so many successful crimes suggested that he had a good mind and knew how to use it.

The caseworkers helped Joe to identify the skills that he'd developed in the criminal world, and showed him how they could be applied to ordinary jobs. It was a revelation to a man who'd despaired of his chances of gaining proper employment on his final release from jail – and who feared that if he didn't get a legitimate job well out of his usual sphere of contacts and friends, he might well be tempted back into the life of crime that had already cost him years in prison and also two of the three key romantic relationships in his life.

Joe had already lost his first serious partner. She'd scarpered pretty swiftly after the time that he had been shot in the head and jaw by police during one of his exploits, sensibly fearing that he was committed to a career in crime and what might happen the next time he ran up against the law. At least, that's how Joe now views her decision to leave. At the time, he was pretty disappointed, but his subsequent criminal career and the headlines across Australia probably confirmed her doubts about his suitability as a long-term partner. Having been shot five times, Joe accepted it as part of his life and knew that any partner would have to understand the risks of his career choice. Joe was back inside Pentridge on sentence when he met the next woman to steal his heart.

Love When Least Expected

Joe met Dawn, a nurse at the time, in the same way that many people meet their life partners – through his younger sister. The difference was that the first time he really noticed her, it wasn't across a nightclub floor, the dinner table or at a local pub, but across a Formica table in the visiting room at Pentridge. Dawn had been dragged along on the visit by Joe's sister, not only to give her someone to talk to during the interminable wait, but also to brighten up Joe's day and give him someone new to talk to besides family. 'Right away, I thought she was a bit of all right', Joe says.

Dawn's first thought when she saw Joe was: 'Oh my, look at those muscles!' He was heavily inked too, but that didn't fuss Dawn. 'Back then, tattoos weren't as common and I thought he looked awesome. Some people might have been intimidated, but I've never worried about things like that. I have a few tattoos myself so I can't talk.'

The next time Dawn and Joe met was on the stairs outside her house. She didn't realise it at the time, but Joe was actually on the run after a prison escape.

> I was pregnant with my second son at the time, and Joe said to me, 'Oooh, you look good pregnant!' I've never forgotten it. I had no idea he was on the run because with young kids and a house to look after, I didn't keep up with the news.

Given Dawn's status as a wife and mother, neither of them had their dating antennae up, but then Dawn's marriage ended.

With Joe in and out of prison, their relationship was never likely to be smooth sailing. One major sticking point was the reaction of some of her family. 'I was warned about Joe, but I always only judged him on how he behaved towards me and my boys. And he was brilliant with the kids – always entertaining them and joking with them.'

It probably didn't help that Dawn's stepfather and stepbrothers were all policemen.

> That led to some interesting family dynamics, I can tell you! When one of my stepbrothers found out who Joe was – one of Australia's most notorious criminals – he said that Joe shouldn't come up to the house any more. But I said that Joe was my life now, and that's just how it was going to be.

By contrast, Dawn's father – a well-educated Dutchman who'd been in the air force and spoke seven languages fluently – was fascinated by his daughter's partner. 'He couldn't believe how intellectual Joe was . . . how well read he was, and how he could discuss anything and everything under the sun.' Much of that education came from Joe's times in prison. For it was there, writing letters, that Joe built both his own knowledge and his relationship with Dawn.

You can get to know a lot about someone from writing letters, Joe says. And you can also learn a lot about your own failings. 'When I first started writing to Dawn, I didn't know an adjective from an adverb. I barely knew what a noun was.' Now he is the author of three books about his life experiences: *Prison Break* and two collections of true-crime stories drawn from his own life.

Having left school at 13, Joe knew that his grip on English wasn't great, but it drove him mad to find that his one way of communicating with his girlfriend – aside from her monthly visits – was hampered by his inability to express his feelings for Dawn in written words. Inside, he secretly managed to get his hands on a dictionary – the *Concise Oxford Dictionary*, to be precise. This he managed to co-opt from a fellow prisoner who was about to be released; to avoid having it confiscated, he disguised it between the covers of another book on Greek literature. Joe then set out to educate himself, reading the dictionary from cover to cover like a novel, one page at a time.

'Writing to Dawn, I also learned how to write in very small letters', Joe says. Back then, prisoners in the Australian system were only allowed to write one-page letters – covering the front and back of a single sheet. As a result, Joe used to squeeze in as much as he could, using tiny writing.

The risk he constantly ran was that prison officers might deem the writing too small. 'If that happened, they'd claim that I was "cheating", and then they'd tell me that that letter could not be sent. Then I'd have to wait a whole other week until I could write to Dawn again.'

'I didn't know that back then', says Dawn today. 'I used to wonder why he wrote in such little writing, and I'd say to him, "My eyesight is good but the magnifying glass makes it clearer!"'

Dawn has kept all of Joe's letters over the years, many of them marked with black lines where 'the screws' (as the prison guards are commonly known) had blacked out a name or possibly a derogatory comment. She thinks that many of the censure marks were probably done out of spite. 'I'm not judgmental usually – I take people at face value until they prove me wrong – but some of the screws were absolutely horrible.'

The ability of prison officers to control access between prisoners and the people they love remains the one thing, out of all the things that he experienced in jail, that still haunts Joe.

It's a mind game every day in there and the main way the prison staff get at you is by manipulating your access to your family. I can still feel the powerlessness, anger and humiliation I felt back then, just talking about it now. Contact with those on the outside is the one little string you have that keeps you sane. But sometimes they used to just withhold letters for no reason at all. Back in the '70s and '80s, prisoners were only allowed a set number of letters per week – it was up to the discretion of prison staff as to which were actually handed over. If you happened to get 10 letters in the one week, you'd only be given three . . . I could just imagine the prison staff going through them and picking out the three most boring ones to give me – not the ones I really wanted and was hanging out for. But you can't complain. If I'd ever complained that I was missing some important letters, then the screws would have had a hold over me. Other times, visiting day would come and they'd call out your name just once, very quietly, so you couldn't hear. Then the officer would go back to the person who'd spent hours travelling to see you and say, 'Well, he didn't come when I called so he obviously doesn't want to see *you*'.

Aside from missing the chance to see Dawn, the worst thing about it was that he knew that she would be left thinking that there was a problem between them. 'It could take a good few letters to sort out even one of those incidents, and it's even worse when you're not a very good letter writer and have trouble saying what you want to say.'

During his years of incarceration – across many different jails and different states – Joe became sensitive to those who were experiencing similar difficulties with their relationships.

'In many cases, their relationship with someone on the outside is the glue that stops those inside from losing it completely. And you can tell when things are going badly – you'd see guys either withdrawing completely, or turning on themselves.'

And should the relationship totally break down – then, Joe says, you knew it was time to steer clear.

You'd see people just crack up and go berserk. I'd see it building up and just keep away, out of the line of fire. Often they'd start mouthing off at the screws, and it would just escalate from there. They'd be begging to be let out so they could go and see her, but of course it never happened.

At the time, Joe considered such behaviour to be a sign of weakness, but he's less sure now. 'The mind games in prison are relentless, so it's no wonder that people crack under the pressure. Some used to talk at great length about what they'd 'do to the bitch' when they got out. Others would clam up completely.'

Of course, as blokes do, they also talked about the good stuff. The worst part of it all, in Joe's mind, were the ones who couldn't stop talking about their kids. Despite being an uncle numerous times over, Joe himself has never had children and couldn't stand listening to the other prisoners going on about theirs. 'I'd just be sitting there nodding and thinking, "I really don't want to hear this shit. I really don't want to hear one more detail about that squirmy little thing".'

But if someone was having an affair with their solicitor – as did happen in at least one case Joe knew of – then everyone soon would know.

'I reckon that guy thought there would be a real advantage in having a solicitor who was really invested in his case. Of course, it came out later that he was playing her along and it didn't last once he got out.'

Joe thinks that some relationships are really just a panacea to help the prisoner get through the long boring days in jail, and it all changes once they're released mainly, as Joe puts it, 'Because then they've got access to the whole lolly shop!'

Joe doesn't have a high opinion of the women – complete strangers – who wrote to him in prison either. 'I never responded to any of them. They'd read about me in the paper and probably thought I sounded exciting.'

And then there were the groupies – women who make a life going from criminal to criminal. 'They get to meet exciting and dangerous people, they never have to pay for anything, and they have access to a lot of inside knowledge.'

One groupie – known as the Black Widow – wrote to Joe. 'She'd been with a number of blokes I knew, and I reckon she thought she had a chance with me. Not a hope.'

Privileges and Punishment

In the confines of jail, it's perhaps understandable that some prisoners reject the outside world and focus completely on their immediate environment and all the associated politics – a self-destructive step, Joe thinks.

> When guys get to that stage, their time is taken up with scheming and planning and trying to better their position inside. They let go of the outside world and only focus on what's in front of them. All their actions and thoughts are directed towards getting more control or more privileges, rather than on what they might do on the outside when they get released.

At times, Joe too felt himself tempted by the privileges that could be earned in prison. But he knew that a prized privilege was also another lever that the screws could use to manipulate him.

> They even offered me a TV at one stage, when TVs were rare and considered a real treat. But I said no, to throw it in the bin. I knew that once I started liking the TV and getting used to having it, then they had the power to take it away from me. It was easier just to do without.

Joe admits that keeping his sense of purpose alive took strength, but that plenty of others managed it too. When every minute of every day is accounted for and every move is carried out under the eye of prison staff, small victories count. It's hard to imagine, but Joe even turned down the chance to earn remission just so that he could keep his beard.

> At the time, it was an offence not to be clean shaven – you could actually be charged if you didn't shave every day! I refused to get

rid of my beard so they told me I wouldn't get any reduction in my sentence, no matter how well I behaved. But you get to the point where you want to have control over *something* in your life, so I stuck to my guns and kept that beard.

At other times, Joe even turned down the chance for a prized prison visit. 'Back then, you were only allowed one visit a month and I've seen guys absolutely torn apart because they've had their visit cancelled. I could see that it was just one more way in which the screws got control, so I just said, "no more visits for me".'

Joe was in maximum security at that time and considered that he had nothing to lose and everything to gain by holding firm. 'Once they knew that they couldn't use the visits against me, and that I didn't care about remission, I was free. It sounds silly placing so much importance on shaving, but at least I could shave whenever I felt like it – not when they did!'

Joe admits that after the prison reforms of previous decades, things are a lot less tough inside now. Indeed, one of Joe's nephews is currently doing time, and Joe can't help but laugh when he hears him complain about how hard it is. 'He has absolutely no idea, but you just can't tell him!' Not that Joe visits his nephew – he knows that he'll be recognised and then there's every chance that the screws will take it out on his nephew.

Of course, some people don't have any option but to immerse themselves in the world of prison. They don't have a partner on the outside to care about how they are doing, when they might get out, and what happens next. But those who do have a partner on the outside also have a fine line to walk, says Joe. 'Your partner is the one thing that keeps you linked to the real world, but you also have to deal with the reality of where you are living.'

In his first book, *Prison Break*, Joe describes the pressures dealt with by every prisoner. 'You have to act abnormally to appear normal in an abnormal situation.' Those who survive time in prison need to have the ability to change when they are released.

> If you internalise the abnormal behaviour, then it's very difficult to adjust on the outside. But if you keep it as a veneer, and shed it when your situation changes, then you have a far better chance. That was me. I could act tough when I needed to, but I also knew what the real me inside was like.

Joe likens the ability to separate his two selves to a guy who is unfailingly polite in front of women but who swears like a trooper in front of his mates. It's all about reading the situation and adjusting to suit the environment. And some people just can't do it.

> Depending on where you are in the jail, in maximum security or one of the other divisions, sometimes you need to step up to your absolute limits of endurance just to survive. Over the years I've seen blokes just crash and burn – they couldn't take the next step up as the pressure was just too much. The screws were always trying to weaken the links in the chain, by taking away privileges or messing around with people's relationships.

Joe firmly believes that the punitive approach doesn't work. 'All it does is send out people who are worse than when they went in. I've seen more than a dozen guys who were released from prison and then went out and killed straight away. Prison distorted their mind so much, they had nothing to lose.'

If Joe hadn't had Dawn waiting on the outside, he suspects he also might have cracked. For many of the years Joe was in prison, Dawn was his touchstone. And even though she ended up leaving him, he still says that she was the best thing that ever happened to him during that time.

Dawn is a genuinely good person – the kind of person who cares about animals and old people and the disabled. She stayed calm, no matter what was going on, she always gave me good advice and she helped me to stay connected to the outside. If I hadn't been with her, I would have taken the whole system on and who knows what would have happened then.

Dawn also opened Joe's eyes to many different ways of looking at the world. Most importantly though, she never nagged him about what he did. 'She just expected that things would change for the better, and eventually they did.'

The Fork in the Road

Before that could happen, Joe had to decide to change. And change wasn't going to be easy given that crime had been his whole life. Like most, he'd started out small, as a teenager on the inner-suburban streets of Brunswick dealing in stolen goods and nicking things for otherwise 'upstanding citizens' who were happy to overlook an item's provenance when it came to getting a cut-price deal. There was easy money to be made, and girlfriends on his arm, and not even a few stints in boys' homes and regular run-ins with the local coppers could dull the appeal of the streets.

At 16, while on the run from a boys' home north of Sydney, Joe and a mate were arrested for trying to steal a car. Banged up in the local lock-up at Orange, a large town in central New South Wales, and bored out of his mind after a few days, the two boys escaped by using their cutlery to saw through the bars in the prison yard. It was to be the first of a number of escapes, some of which made front-page news across the country.

Just a few months later, he was back behind bars – Pentridge this time – with the magistrate deciding that a stolen car, a few break-ins and his previous escape from the lock-up at Orange meant that Joe was deserving of an adult prison, despite his young age. And that's where his real education in crime began.

In his book, *Australian True Crime Stories: Real-life Tales from an Ex-Con*, Joe describes settling into prison life:

> Within a week I had a job helping in the hospital here, or recovery ward, as it was called. There was a passing parade of sick or injured crims from all the other divisions in Pentridge with time on their hands, bored, with lots of stories to tell. And I was a willing, impressionable young mind, open to all that was on offer. In the hierarchy of prison, I quickly learned that at the top, safe-breakers were equal to bank-robbers, but violent crime didn't appeal to me, even though it was evident that it was easier and generated almost as much money as safes. By the end of my short sentence, I left prison determined to be a safe-breaker. So began my descent into serious crime.

One of Joe's fellow prisoners during his early days in Pentridge was Ronald Ryan, who went on to be the last person to be hanged in Victoria. To Joe's annoyance at the time, Ryan resolutely refused to share his knowledge of safe-breaking with him, suggesting instead that he try getting a real job. Joe now regrets that he ignored this advice.

Today, Joe sees his decision like a fork in the road – faced with the choice of turning left or right, he deliberately chose the dark side.

Crooked Cops and Black Money

Joe still takes pride in the fact that he was never charged with offences against civilians.

In jail in Queensland, Joe remembers meeting one man who'd raped a girl, stabbed her 17 times and left her for dead in a ditch.

Somehow the girl had found the strength to crawl out, reach help, and then, after months of rehabilitation, to turn up at court to give evidence against her attacker.

I looked at this guy and thought: 'Why is a man like him in the same yard as me? How does his crime possibly compare with mine?' The man started giving Joe some dirty looks and Joe swiftly set him straight: 'Don't for a minute start thinking you're tough because you stabbed some innocent girl 17 times'. What a scumbag! I'd rather go hungry than target someone innocent. I always went after the black money – people who'd made money out of ripping others off.

In fact, Joe says corrupt police were his favourite target.

Back in the 1970s, the police force was riddled with corruption. You'd be hard pressed to find one copper in a squad who wasn't on the take – and I should know, I had more than a few of them on my payroll over the years. My partner used to target police who'd retired early. They were the ones who'd been as crooked as, and who had lots of money. It made sense to take it away from them – who were they going to complain to, if their stolen money was then stolen from them?

In all, Joe spent about 10 years in prison – not counting time spent on remand waiting for his day in court. Back then, days spent in remand were not counted towards a final prison sentence, an injustice that thankfully has been righted with reforms.

'These days it's much fairer', says Joe. 'One day locked up is treated as one day locked up. Once you could wait six or seven months on remand and if you eventually went down, none of that time on remand counted as time served.'

Still, it was a lot more time than Joe ever planned on spending behind bars. Part of it was happenstance – being caught for things that he had done. But Joe also had his share of dodgy charges.

Joe reckons that of all the times he was convicted, about 11 were for crimes he had not committed. On the flipside, he also came across people in jail who were doing time for *his* crimes. He was generally happy to set the record straight, saying: 'You know that charge you went down on – that was actually one of mine!'

But if the cops were corrupt, they were also lazy. One time, Joe came across a guy who'd been charged with an offence that was eerily similar to one of the dud ones for which Joe was now serving time. 'Reading his paperwork, I realised that the arresting officer was not only the same bloke who'd got me, but the copper *hadn't even bothered changing the story.*'

Years later, Joe heard from a biker friend that he knew where that cop was living. The biker had a cunning plan to letterbox the street with copies of Joe's book – which detailed the cop's corrupt activities – so that all his neighbours would know that he was far from being the honest citizen he appeared. Tempting as it was, Joe didn't go along with the plot.

Joe does make a fine distinction between corruption and expediency. 'A lot of deals go on behind the scenes with the Director of Public Prosecutions – sometimes they'd reduce the sentence if you were prepared to plead guilty, or perhaps they'd charge you with a lesser offence.'

In Joe's view, it was more about strategy and saving money than true justice. But when he found himself in prison again on the basis of evidence that the police had fabricated, he was determined to escape.

Escape and Its Aftermath

As Joe puts it, most prisoners don't try to escape because failure can be painful and they run the risk of being killed; however, Joe was mad as hell at being set up and decided he had nothing to lose. And he had good friends on the outside – the type of friends who were prepared to risk their own lives and break *into* prison to bust him out.

> Everyone in jail says that they are innocent, but I really did believe that I should only be convicted on real evidence – and not on evidence that the police concocted. If I'm in here, I should be in here for my own stupidity, not because some copper thinks, 'Hey, Joe's gotta be guilty of something – let's lock him up!'

On 28 June 1980, two men entered Yatala Prison's maximum security block, B-Division, and used a blowtorch to help free Joe from his third-floor cell.

It was a bold escape, and police lost no time in setting up a taskforce to hunt him down. 'With a lot of escapes, they don't worry too much – they just keep an eye on the family home and wait for you to turn up or one of your mates to dob you in. It's just another job for them.' But Joe's escape was declared a major crime, and a separate squad was established to recapture him. Despite the resources thrown at the problem, Joe and his unknown, unnamed friends seemed to have vanished.

While on the run, Joe had no direct contact with friends. Instead, he used to post letters to his sister and she would then forward them on to whomever he wanted to contact. 'The funny thing was that I was in Queensland at that stage, but my sister thought I was in Melbourne, so told everyone I was in Queensland! That was a little too close to the truth!'

Again, Joe's friends came through and helped keep him informed of what the police were thinking and doing. At one stage, he heard that they thought he was trying to get a passport to flee the country. 'But only an imbecile would want to leave Australia. It's a brilliant country, and you can survive perfectly well with nothing in your pocket if you have to.'

A paid contact on the police force sent him copies of the *Commonwealth Gazette*, which gave him useful information on progress into the investigation. In the end, Joe's eventual capture was an anticlimax. Police turned up at his rented house in north Queensland looking for the previous tenant. Little did they expect to find the subject of a nationwide taskforce. Joe was back behind bars.

From his time on the run, Joe was charged with many offences. The trial dragged on for 54 days, and over 80 witnesses were called, one of whom was the Commissioner of Police (who later served 12 years himself for crimes of corruption). Of the 23 charges, Joe was convicted of just five. Some were unproven; others had been dropped when Joe was able to prove he'd been elsewhere at the time.

'A few of the charges related to some robberies of police stations, but the police had never reported them – actually, how would you report a robbery to yourself? – so they had to be dropped', Joe explains. In the end, he was given a sentence of six years to be served in Queensland. And then he'd be sent back to South Australia to face charges relating to the escape there.

The Riot

A Queensland jail in the 1980s was not a pleasant place to be. And while staff were perfectly happy running an 18th-century-style prison, the prisoners were determined to drag them into the 20th century.

Now incarcerated in Queensland, Joe became caught up in a major prison riot – sparked by the appalling prison conditions. 'Unlike what you read in the paper, 20 guys isn't a riot, it's a skirmish', he says. 'But this one was the real deal.'

After the riot was over, Joe was accused of being one of the ringleaders, but as he puts it, it is impossible to lead a riot. 'You can give advice or plan something – we'll do this, and then we'll ask for that. Strategic planning, if you will. But by their nature, riots are uncontrollable. They just erupt.'

Joe still remembers prison staff literally reading them the Riot Act – an official statement that, once read, allowed prison staff to operate under a whole new book of law. A bit like the Terrorism Act, it essentially allowed them to shoot first and ask questions later. 'But one of the key things about the Riot Act is that it has to be heard and acknowledged. So you've got prison staff reading it out, and prisoners yelling and screaming and doing their bit to ignore it. One bloke was even throwing shit at them.'

Eventually, the riot was quelled and the four men who were thought to be behind it were thrown into a new multimillion-dollar maximum-security facility that had only just been built. Now it was home to four prisoners, and four double squads of screws to look after them. But Dawn didn't know this at the time. She didn't know whether Joe was dead or alive, injured or unharmed. For three days, she pestered and nagged prison authorities to see Joe. Then on the fourth day, in utter desperation, she convinced a journalist at Brisbane's *Courier Mail* to accompany her to the prison. There she threatened the staff that if she wasn't allowed in, she'd give the full story to the papers.

She isn't sure whether it was this threat, her persistence or sympathy for her plight, but Dawn was finally allowed in – right into the heart of maximum security. 'I sat in the hallway between the cells holding the other prisoners and talked to him. At last I knew that he was alive and OK. Some of the others had been horribly beaten though.'

As Dawn was being ushered out, the guard warned her that if she ever told anyone she'd been allowed inside, they would all deny it as it was completely against the law. 'But I didn't care what the consequences were – I just had to see that Joe was alive', she says. Joe's admiration for her is clear.

> She'd come all the way up from Melbourne to visit me, and you wouldn't believe the bullshit they put her through. But she just wouldn't give in, just kept on repeating that she was here to see me until finally they gave in. Later, I heard all the obstacles they tried to put in her way, and I knew that I would have given up long before then. She is a remarkable woman.

The time following the prison riot was one of the lowest points in Joe's life. 'If Dawn hadn't been there for me, I don't know where my life would have gone. I was hammered mentally.'

Some of Joe's fellow prisoners had been so badly beaten that they required hospitalisation, but he was never assaulted physically. 'I think it was because I had the balls to say to them, "If any of you touch me, I will get your family".' Joe still remembers turning around to face the prison officers, so that he could see the person silly enough to throw the first punch. Then he told them that he didn't have much money, but that he would spend it wisely and their families would suffer.

> I could see that they really wanted to hammer me, but they knew I had people on the outside, which very few people have. Most prisoners might have friends or family who'll send money or a book or come for a visit, but very few have the kind of friends who might be prepared to hunt someone down on the outside.

The fact that Joe's friends on the outside had risked death to break him out of Yatala in South Australia was probably enough to give the prison officers pause. He survived the riot and its aftermath without a scratch.

Return to South Australia

Once his sentence in Queensland had been served, Joe was extradited back to South Australia where he faced more charges relating to his escape from Yatala Prison. However, he was fortunate to be charged with escape under the most recent laws and not under the laws in place at the time of the actual offence. It was a simple mistake, but the result was that not a single day was added to his original sentence.

'They [the police] were so pissed off that they then threatened that I'd lose all of my remissions. But I knew the police were still desperate to find who'd helped me escape, so I told the governor that if I didn't get my remissions back, I'd name *him* as the person who helped me.' Joe doesn't think his threat seriously worked, but a few days later he was told that yes, all his remissions had been reinstated.

Being considered a flight risk, Joe was now back in maximum security; his only link to the outside world was the regular visits from Dawn. By then, she'd moved her young family across from Victoria so she could be closer to Joe for the chance of an hour's visit once a week or a fortnight – 'whatever the screws decided to give us'.

Sometimes Dawn had the children with her too. She'd been reluctant to take them with her at first, until she knew what the atmosphere would be like, but then she relented. 'They looked forward to visiting Joe even more than I did if that's possible.'

Only a few people would be granted access each week, and Dawn found herself sitting outside the prison at 5.30 am just to give herself the best chance of being at the head of the queue. 'Sometimes I'd sit there for five or six hours in the freezing cold, only for the screws to come out and say, "You can't see him because he's been a bad boy this week". I don't know how many times that happened', says Dawn.

Even when she did get in to see Joe, Dawn says that the experience was overwhelming. 'Most people have never been into a prison and heard the door slamming behind them. That's scary enough, but as a visitor, you know that you'll be out of there in an hour while your partner has to stay behind. It's heartbreaking, and not an experience you can easily describe.'

There was no such thing as a conjugal visit, and even holding hands depended on the mood of the guard at the time – some were prepared to look the other way, but Joe and Dawn knew that the couldn't push it. 'We'd be in a tiny grungy little cell with a screw listening to every word we said.' Often the guards would taunt Dawn by asking what a nice girl like her was doing with a bloke like Joe and they'd invite her to go out with them instead. 'They were probably trying to get a rise out of Joe, but they'd never succeed. Joe didn't give a shit – he would just bide his time to get back at them', she says.

Once Dawn had arranged a contact visit to coincide with Joe's birthday, but when she got there the guards informed them that it wasn't going to happen. Instead, she found herself facing Joe through glass again. 'I looked at him and I had tears in my eyes, and I remember saying to him, "This isn't a fucking life".'

Brothers in Adversity

In prison, not everyone is a bad person, says Joe. 'Sure, most people in prison have done bad things, but when you meet a truly evil person, it is a completely different matter. I've met absolute evil and, believe me, it will make you cringe. People like that need to either stay in prison forever or be exterminated.'

Some people try to big note themselves and suffer the consequences. While it was an offence to ask what others prisoners were in for, word soon spread – sometimes true, sometimes not. Joe had a contact in prison administration who was able to get him access to prisoner files, so he was able to tell whether or not they were lying. 'If they were lying, you knew they had a hidden agenda, and then they'd get flogged.'

Revenge could take many forms and not even being in protection could necessarily save you. Joe was in prison with Mark 'Chopper' Read at one point, when Chopper was put in protection. 'Chopper claimed it was to keep others safe from him, but it wasn't. There were plenty of people who wanted to get him.'

It's not like how people imagine. In prison, it's not about fighting one on one. If someone is too physically strong, then three people will take him down. Best of all is if you set something up so that you're not even there when it happens. That way you can avoid the risk of getting seriously hurt. Instead of getting in a direct fight, you work out some other way to get them, and trust me, there are plenty of other ways.'

In one case, Joe remembers being pissed off by a bloke who was needlessly throwing his weight around. One of Joe's mates told him that the guy had already stepped on a number of toes and not to worry about it – he wouldn't last long. 'Sure enough, someone put a booby-trapped cigarette lighter on his locker and he just couldn't resist – he flicked it and bang! Half of his fingers and one of his eyes went, just like that. The bastard was taken out of there in minutes.' Joe and his mates just hoped that they would get someone more congenial next time.

Dobbers also get short shrift in prison, although Joe can understand why someone might tell a lie to gain some advantage.

At one stage, police had been told that Joe was part of some nationwide gang and had a special tattoo that would confirm his membership. He was ordered to strip. 'I didn't know what it was all about, so at first I refused, but then they insisted that the orders came right from the very top. So I did a deal with them: if they'd tell me what it was about, and I thought it sounded legit, then I'd cooperate totally.'

Joe couldn't help but laugh when he heard that they were looking for a tattoo of a star with dots, or something equally ridiculous. 'I happily stripped and let them have a look, but really, it was all bullshit. Someone had just made the whole story up to get privileges.'

Another guy Joe knew went to the trouble of having bullets smuggled into prison – not to make a gun, in fact, but to use as currency with the screws. 'He went to them and said that he'd found the bullets and someone was obviously trying to make a gun. The guards thought he was a hero, of course, and he got sent to a nice country prison instead. It's all about tactics.'

Joe himself found a bullet in his cell one day. Thinking he'd been set up and worried about the consequences should it be found in a random search, he swallowed it. He spent the next few days worrying about its reappearance.

Cleaning the Slate

Joe was finally released from prison in 1988, and he moved in with Dawn and her two boys. It was the first time they'd lived together as a family unit.

'If I hadn't been with Dawn, I most likely would have failed again', says Joe. 'It's very hard to keep straight. You go from that world to this world, and making the transition is unbelievably hard.'

Dawn also had to make the transition to having Joe around full-time.

> It may sound odd, but the hardest part was the fact that I couldn't go to the shop or the toilet or anywhere without him being close behind me, like a shadow. I'd go to the supermarket, and reach up to grab something, only to find his hand in the pocket of my jeans. It wasn't possessiveness. I think it was the fact that he'd been locked up for so many years without proper human contact, and he really needed it.

For the first few months of Joe's freedom, they lived 'looking over our shoulders and out the windows at night', says Dawn. 'We were raided by police several times but nothing was found and after a while they didn't bother anymore.'

Having grown up in a strict household, Dawn was equally strict in her own home. That meant definitely no guns – her greatest fear – and no stolen goods. 'There is enough violence out on the streets without inviting it into your home. And I never wanted anyone to be able to walk into our house and say that we had stolen property there.'

Dawn doesn't think she nagged Joe too much about going straight, but she admits she probably made it clear that she wouldn't stay around if he went back to his old ways. 'I just wanted him to have a normal life – playing with the kids, having a dog, riding our bikes and having fun. All the little everyday things he'd missed out on for so long.'

For 18 months they led the normal life that both Dawn and Joe had craved, but there was one cloud hanging over them. Joe still had an extradition order from 16 years earlier when he'd broken parole in Victoria. He was free to live in South Australia, but not to leave the state or he'd face prison again.

Dawn was of the firm view that they could be perfectly happy living in South Australia for the rest of their lives, but Joe was adamant that he wanted to be free to travel anywhere in Australia. Knowing that he still had a prison sentence hanging over his head was no kind of life.

Joe's decision to return to Victoria and face the music was a defining moment in their relationship. 'Dawn saw that I'd made a unilateral decision to surrender myself. I didn't talk to her about it – I already knew what she would say, as she'd said it so many times before.'

As Dawn describes it, Joe's decision to return to Victoria led to some of the darkest days of her life. 'I knew he was going back to jail and there was nothing I could do about it. He could have stayed in South Australia but he didn't want to have to worry about being arrested if he crossed the border.' Nowadays Dawn says that she can understand his reasoning. 'At the time, it was probably selfish of me to say that I didn't want him to go back to jail. When you're happy, you don't want to lose it. But I had to respect his decision.'

With the help of his lawyer and an understanding magistrate, Joe made arrangements to surrender himself to police at Horsham in Victoria. Dawn was with him for his final moments of freedom, then returned back to South Australia.

Joe had a 10-month sentence for the parole violation. And no-one could have been more surprised than Joe at the reception he got when he finally arrived back at Pentridge.

The screw who greeted me had been a total rat when I'd been in there before, but now it was like he'd discovered a better self. He greeted me like a long-lost friend, complained about how all the prisoners these days were druggies and losers. Then he said, 'Pick your prison! Where do you want to serve out your time?

116

Give me your word that you'll behave and I'll see you right'. I thought Jesus – now you're prepared to take MY word?

Joe found out that some of his old friends – lifers he'd known at the start of their sentences – were at a prison in the country, so asked to be transferred there, not ever believing it would actually happen. But his new-found screw buddy was as good as his word, and Joe spent the rest of his sentence – his final sentence – among good friends and with a degree of freedom he'd never experienced in prison before. 'It was more like a holiday camp than prison – we had a great time.'

For a while, Dawn kept up a punishing regime of prison visits – working all week then leaving on the Friday night for the long drive to Victoria. She'd visit Joe for a couple of hours on Saturday and Sunday, then return to Adelaide. 'I could only do it twice a month, and had to budget really hard to afford it, because I was only on a part pension and a small wage', says Dawn.

Dawn is one of those people with a gift for friendship, still having many of the friends she first made when she moved to Melbourne as a skinny 17 year old from Brisbane – and these friends rallied around her now. 'A few friends who were truck drivers would give me a lift over to Melbourne when they could. And then a girlfriend in Melbourne would loan me her car so I could drive to Sale to see Joe.'

It was difficult being separated again – this time by Joe's own choice to surrender himself – but the real crunch came for Dawn when one of her sons gave her an ultimatum: him or Joe.

Joe would never say it, but that was the real reason we finally broke up. My son had been living with his father, but now said that if I stopped seeing Joe, he'd move back to live with me and his brother. I chose having my kids together again, even though my son probably would have been perfectly fine staying with his father. My son has always been quite a jealous person. Maybe I should have seen his behaviour then for what it was. But who knows what lies ahead on the road; you just carry along it the best you can at the time.

Joe was distraught at the end of their relationship, but what really stung was hearing from a friend that Dawn had fled to Queensland, fearing that Joe would be incredibly angry.

When I heard that I was completely shocked. I was like 'What?' I couldn't believe that Dawn thought that I would do her any harm. Although she dumped me, not even that could wipe out all the good parts of the times we shared together. Besides, that's not the kind of man I am. Even though I was devastated, I could still be objective . . . I could understand why she left me.

As Dawn tells it, a mutual friend had warned her that Joe would come after her on his release, and Dawn had believed her. 'I'd been through a rotten break-up, I was insecure at the time, and I really needed my mum and my family home back in Brisbane.'

Yet after a while, Dawn had the urge to head back to Melbourne. 'One day, I just decided that I didn't want to run any more.' Nervous but determined, Dawn left the kids with a friend in Melbourne and went to the home of one of Joe's sisters. 'I thought to myself that maybe I'll never go home from here. If Joe wants to kill me he can, but at least my kids are safe.'

Joe is still horrified that Dawn could have thought such a thing – he would even have been happy to leave the state so that she could feel comfortable coming back to Melbourne – but now he had a chance to set the record straight.

When I knocked on Joe's sister's door and the door opened and I saw Joe standing there, I instantly knew I would be all right. Joe didn't look evil or mean, he just gave me a loving look as if to say all will be OK, and to this day he is one of my closest and dearest friends. This friendship will last a lifetime.

These days, nothing would tempt Joe back into doing anything that might land him behind bars again. 'I gave crime my best shot and failed miserably. The gang I was up against was far more capable, far better resourced *and* it was backed by the government. I couldn't win. So I decided to take on a different challenge – to take on a job with the government.' But before Joe landed the role of caretaker on the island, he went back to prison on a number of occasions – as a guest speaker no less.

'I don't know whether I did any good or not, but I gave it a shot.' Joe used to talk to prisoners about the decisions he'd made and the consequences he'd faced. He likens a life in crime to driving a car – not something you should do without knowing the road rules.

They'd all nod at that and then I'd ask them something about law and they wouldn't know. Then I'd say, 'See. You're in the car and you don't know the road rules. Get out of the car right now! I wasn't there to try and talk them out of a life in crime. I used to say if you really want it, go for it! You might make some money if you're any good. But if you're caught, you'll do time and nothing is worth that – not even a million dollars.

It wasn't until Joe started writing about his life that he realised what had driven him all those years. In fact, it hadn't been the money, but the gamble. (Even in prison, gambling was rife and it wasn't unusual for bets of $10,000 to be placed. That's $30,000 in today's money, but unsurprisingly, given the company, debts were always honoured.)

For Joe, the real appeal of a life in crime was the adrenalin rush that came with living on his wits and outsmarting his enemies. Even when he had plenty of money, he was constantly chasing the next buzz.

These days though, he gets it through his job – as an accredited firefighter who has helped fight major fires across three states, an advanced fire-line tree feller, and a 4×4 instructor and chainsaw trainer. But it's at his regular place of work – one of Victoria's national parks – that he's most at home. He may not have a million dollars, but he enjoys million-dollar views every day.

One thing he has lost is his old mates. Joe felt guilty about cutting off contact with the guys who'd been through so much with him, but knew that if he was to have any chance of a normal life, he needed to get away from anyone who was still active in the underworld. 'I didn't even want to hear what they were up to, in case I got dragged back into it. Even just having knowledge of a crime could be enough.'

Dawn, too, has nothing to do with the criminal world, although she still laughs over one incident in recent years.

I was at a party and people were talking about which crims they knew. Someone mentioned that Joe's nephew had recently been sent to prison, and a guy called Brian started saying how he knew Joe really well, and had spent a lot of time with Joe and his missus and her kids. I just sat there listening as Brian was going on about what a good cook she was and how he used to hang out at Joe's house all the time, and then I asked: 'So you know her well then?' He said that Joe's partner hadn't been a bad sort, and it was then I finally said, *'Well, how come I've never seen you before in my life?'* You've never seen a bloke disappear quite so quickly!

In fact, Joe and Dawn are still in regular contact and remain great mates. Dawn is unbelievably proud of what Joe has achieved, the man he has become and how he has turned his life around, although Joe insists that she's far too generous in her opinion of him after all the shit he put her through. Today, Dawn is happily repartnered, and Joe also has a new partner, Julie. Julie knows all about his past, and is understanding of some of his foibles – the result of years spent looking over one shoulder.

'Pain is a good teacher, and I've been well and truly programmed by it', says Joe. Even today, Joe finds it impossible to sit with his back to a door. 'I find it creepy. Although I know it's foolish and that no-one these days is going to come and get me, it has happened in the past and old habits die hard. I can't relax unless I can see the door and a way out.'

Chapter 5
Lady Killers

Most of us look for a lack of a criminal record when searching for love, but there are others who are drawn to 'bad' boys like pins to a magnet. And the more high profile the crime, the more attractive the perpetrator to some suitors. Indeed, men serving time for some of the most heinous of acts appear to have enough sex appeal to turn prison into a veritable lovers' lane.

The Lovers' Escape

Pretty prison warden falls for muscled con.

For the Australian public in 1993, it sounded like a plot lifted straight from the long-running *Prisoner* TV series of the previous decade. But it was real-life, headline news. For 27-year old Heather Dianne Parker, her workplace romance caused the death of one man and changed the lives of many others irrevocably.

Parker's childhood had been hell, thanks to her alcoholic father. She ran away from home as soon as she could, and at 17 she married a fellow prison officer, Mick Parker. Practically before she'd left her own childhood behind, Heather Parker was a wife and a mother to two children of her own.

A decade on, Parker was tempted, like so many others, by the charms and attention of someone she met at work. Except in this case, it was not a flirtation with a co-worker, but with one of her charges: 38-year-old Peter Robert Gibb, a man who'd spent only 22 months out of prison since he was 17.

In 1992, the dark, well-built and tattooed Gibb was being held in the Melbourne Remand Centre on Spencer Street, for armed robbery. Gibb was in great physical shape, thanks to his obsession with exercise, and had perfected a tough line of talk in various prisons. Perhaps it was boredom with her marriage, or perhaps it was his muscled physique and thick dark hair, but Parker found Gibb irresistible.

The pair struck up a flirtation, which soon grew physical. No longer content with a quick kiss when Parker opened Gibb's cell in the mornings, the two began seeking greater privacy. Needless to say, any fraternising between prison staff and prisoners was against the rules, so in May 1992, when Parker and Gibbs were seen on a security video sneaking into a broom cupboard together, there was uproar. Parker was transferred away from the Remand Centre and before long she'd also left her marriage.

Exactly what sparked the audacious plan is unknown, but two days before Gibb escaped, he had been sentenced to 12 years with a minimum of 10 years. Perhaps the pair decided that tear-soaked letters would not be enough to sustain them for the next decade. Gibb wanted out, and the besotted Parker was only too happy to help. (Ironically, the conviction for which Gibb was in prison this time was later overturned on appeal. Had he been a little more patient, he could have simply walked out the front door.)

It was supposedly impossible for anyone to escape from the Melbourne Remand Centre, but Gibb had serious form, both as a violent armed robber and, tellingly, as a (briefly) successful escapee. Also along for the ride was Gibb's new best friend from Unit 5 of the Remand Centre – career criminal Archie Butterly.

The whole escape was meticulously planned, but even today, the full extent of Parker's involvement is unknown. It is thought that Parker organised a contact to steal a couple of getaway vehicles and false number plates. She kitted out the four-wheel drive with everything they would need for life on the run: camping gear, police scanners, food and petrol supplies, mobile phones, bolt-cutters, handcuffs, a camouflage net and even a machine for cutting keys. This car was stashed in a storage unit near Frankston. A second car, equipped with a gun, was left near the prison for their getaway. But first Gibb and Butterly had to escape.

Their plan was to go out with a bang – quite literally. A small piece of explosive was smuggled into the prison (perhaps Parker again) and at about 6 pm on Sunday, 7 March, Gibb and Butterly used it to blow out one of the reinforced windows. With the glass gone, the pair used knotted, prison-issue sheets to lower themselves down onto LaTrobe Street.

The alarm had been sounded, and although the pair managed to get away in the car Parker had left, they were followed by a prison guard who flagged down a passing taxi. It was a true-life case of a 'follow that car' moment from a movie.

The escapees floored their car, driving at high speed down Footscray Road and screaming through red traffic lights. Not even a minor bingle with another car on the corner of Flinders Street slowed them down, but then they crashed the car more seriously. Butterly was badly injured, Gibb less so, but both managed to clamber free of the wreckage. A passing Samaritan on a motorbike got the shock of his life when he stopped to help, only to have his bike stolen at gunpoint. Gibbs drove, with Butterly riding pillion.

It was Moomba Sunday, just on dusk, and all hell had broken loose. Across the radio, all police cars were being rallied to the chase. On Southbank Boulevard, the escaping pair crashed again, Gibb proving himself just as inept at driving a motorbike as a car. Senior Constables Warren Treloar and John Schoenpflug from the Prahran police station were first to arrive on the scene. Not seeing the gun, Treloar leapt out and struck Gibb with his baton, breaking his arm. Then, without warning, Butterly shot Treloar twice, in his shoulder and chest. The bullet hit just above the heart, causing his lungs to collapse. Gibb leaned over and grabbed Treloar's service revolver from its holster. Now faced with two guns, Schoenpflug could do nothing as the two prisoners leaped into the police van and sped off. An Australia-wide alert was issued, warning that the escapees were armed and extremely dangerous.

In the meantime, the pair was joined by Parker and the trio picked up the four-wheel drive and fled Melbourne for the bush. But they were not in good shape. Gibb's left arm was broken, and Butterly had sustained internal injuries from the car crash. They stopped at the La Trobe Valley Hospital in Gippsland for care, and for once their luck held, with no-one recognising them. Patched up, they then went into hiding in the spectacular alpine region of northeastern Victoria.

Gibb's desire to romance Parker with a night out on the town proved to be their undoing. Against the wishes of Butterly, on Thursday, 11 March, Parker and Gibb checked into a hotel in the historic hamlet of Gaffney's Creek. Butterly was very unwell, so they smuggled him into the hotel room where he could rest more comfortably. Gibb and Parker had a romantic dinner in the hotel dining room among unsuspecting locals, and took extra food back to the room for Butterly, who was still losing serious amounts of blood from his injuries.

Realising that the blood was a dead giveaway that something suspicious had gone on in the room, the three crept away in the middle of the night. By the next morning, the historic hotel had gone up in flames. It was either one heck of a coincidence or the three had decided to cover their tracks by burning the bloodied love nest down.

Police coming to check out the fire were soon told about the couple who'd stayed the night before and were given a description of their car. The focus of the hunt was now centred on the northeastern region, with more than 50 police being brought in to set up road blocks, and check out campsites, huts and bush tracks.

On Saturday, 13 March, nearly a week after the great escape, a couple of bushwalkers happened across the four-wheel drive, near a peaceful spot named Picnic Point, outside Jamieson. Tracker dogs were brought in to sniff out the fugitives who, police reasoned, would not have strayed far from their one means of transport.

About 700 metres from the road, a sniffer dog found their campsite, but the gang had either heard the dog approach or the police creeping through the bush. At 2 pm, a firefight erupted. Hundreds of shots were fired from a submachine gun and other high-powered weapons. Just one policeman was hit in the leg, but plenty of others described the sensation of bullets whizzing past their heads. The battle lasted half an hour, then Gibb and Parker were spotted making a run for it – or rather, a wade for it – through the Goulburn River. Parker raised her arms above her head signaling that they were ready to surrender.

Butterly was found hidden in a clump of bushes, surrounded by a sleeping bag, food and drink, and an armoury's worth of weapons. There was a single bullet hole behind his left ear. At first it was thought that the fatal wound was from a lucky shot from police during the barrage. But later, forensic experts at Parker and Gibb's committal hearing would explain to the court that Butterly had been shot in the head by the revolver that Gibb had stolen from Senior Constable Treloar. The gunshot residue found on Butterly's hands was not consistent with suicide, and the question still remains: was it Parker or Gibb who killed Butterly? Neither has ever talked.

At their trial, both were convicted of 40 offences relating to the escape. Murder was not one of them. As the coroner said in the inquest into Butterly's death: 'Whether Butterly took his own life after firing a limited number of rounds at police or he was shot by Gibb or Parker essentially will remain unanswered'.

At sentencing, Parker's counsel told Mr Justice Joseph O'Shea that Parker was motivated by love and felt no remorse. Both were given 10-year sentences, later reduced on appeal. Gibb was released in 1997, and six months later, in September, rolled up in a stretch limousine to collect Parker on her release from Deer Park Prison. They celebrated their reunion with a night at the Crown Towers.

But there was to be no 'happy ever after' for Parker and Gibb. Parker had difficulty finding work. Gibb returned to his old ways and spent a brief time back in jail for theft. Parker, too, faced the Ringwood Court in 2005, and was fined $1500 for handling stolen property.

On the home front, things were not blissful either, despite the fact that Gibb and Parker now had two children of their own. There were tales of heavy drinking, violence and a string of other women. In 2007, Parker appeared in the County Court for attacking one of Gibb's girlfriends. At the trial, Parker's lawyer said that his client was still living with Gibb, but that she described their relationship as sometimes being a 'living hell'. He told the court Parker made one of the biggest mistakes of her life when she helped Gibb escape, and that she was still haunted by the stigma of the breakout. Parker only received a suspended sentence for the attack, but despite everything Parker and Gibb had done to be with each other, the pair separated soon after.

In January 2012, Peter Robert Gibb died after being assaulted at his Melbourne home. In a violent and twisted version of the incident from best-selling local book *The Slap*, Gibb was beaten up by three men after placing a child in a freezer during a party. He claimed it was a drunken prank, and that the child was only inside for a couple of seconds, but it was a practical joke that was to cost him his life. Gibb was admitted to hospital in the early hours of the morning, and by 6 am he was dead. An autopsy revealed he had had a long-term heart condition. No charges were laid against the men who spurred on his death. It's not known whether Heather Parker celebrated or mourned the death of her prison lover.

The Night Stalker

In 1985, the people of Los Angeles county were under a virtual state of siege, thanks to the night-time rampages of self-confessed Satanist, Richard Ramirez. Scared by almost daily headlines, people would obsessively check their locks, close their windows, and forbid access to anyone who was unknown to them. But no matter what precautions the people of Los Angeles county took, it wasn't enough to keep the Night Stalker out.

Over the course of one long, oppressively hot summer, Ramirez prowled the suburbs and broke into numerous people's homes, brutally attacking anyone he found with guns, knives and hammers before raping and murdering them. Many of the crimes were signed with a pentagram – drawn in blood on the walls or on the thighs of the victims.

On 30 August 1985, an arrest warrant for Richard Ramirez was issued and his face made the front page of the day's newspapers. Unaware that his identity was now public knowledge, Ramirez was returning from visiting his brother in Tucson, Arizona. Getting off the Greyhound bus, he popped into a liquor store, where he was recognised by a worker who'd seen his face in the newspaper. Shocked by the woman's screams, Ramirez fled the store and began running, but the store worker's cries attracted attention and a small mob gathered and set off in pursuit.

In desperation, Ramirez tried to steal a car, not noticing that the owner was actually lying on a trolley underneath it doing some repairs. When Ramirez started the engine, the man pulled out from beneath the car and also began chasing Ramirez. The growing mob eventually caught up with Ramirez and began beating him with steel bars before the police arrived and arrested him. He was charged with 43 counts in total, including 13 murders and numerous other charges of burglary, sodomy and rape.

As the Manson trial had done some years before, the Night Stalker trial attracted a crowd of groupies who hung around the courthouse dressed in black robes, chanting messages of support. On 20 September 1989, the Night Stalker, Richard Ramirez, was found guilty of all 43 counts and sentenced to death for each murder. On hearing his sentence, he simply shrugged and said, 'Big deal. Death always came with the territory'.

Sitting on death row, Ramirez was swamped with love letters from women. But it was a 41-year-old freelance magazine editor, Doreen Lioy, who caught his attention. Maybe it was the 75 letters she wrote to him that finally wore him down. Or maybe it was the fact that she claimed to be a virgin (and probably still is, given that death-row prisoners are not allowed the privilege of conjugal visits). In any case, the Night Stalker and Doreen Lioy were married by the prison chaplain in the visiting room at San Quentin Prison on 3 October 1996. Witnesses at the wedding included one journalist and some of America's most dangerous men. Ramirez' wedding ring was silver – Satanic worshippers are not allowed to wear gold. To this day, Ramirez remains on death row, with no execution date yet set.

The Charismatic Killer

He had sex with putrefying corpses until they disintegrated, decapitated at least 12 victims and kept some of the heads in his apartment as souvenirs. By any sane person's reckoning, Ted Bundy seems an unlikely choice for Mr Right. However, not only was he a necrophiliac, rapist, kidnapper, foot fetishist and serial killer, Ted Bundy also became a husband, marrying Carol Ann Boone in a bizarre court ceremony in Florida.

Born in a home for unwed mothers in 1948, Ted Bundy grew up to be both handsome and charming – two key traits that helped him lure more than 30 young women to their deaths. Often feigning injury or a disability, or posing as an authority figure – policeman, fireman, inspector – Bundy would approach his victims in a public place, then overpower them and take them somewhere more secluded where he would alternately strangle, stab or bludgeon them. Or he'd simply break into random houses and beat his victims to death while they slept.

As well as being good-looking, the young Bundy was smart too – he was an honours student in psychology, and worked at the Seattle Suicide Hotline crisis centre before swapping over to law, and he also worked on various political campaigns in Washington. However Bundy began skipping his university classes and then stopped attending altogether. In hindsight, it's probably no coincidence that his sudden lack of interest in study coincided with the time that young women began disappearing across the north-west US (an area that includes the states of Washington and Oregon), but his tutors weren't to know for some time exactly why their star student's attention had wandered.

No-one knows exactly when Bundy began killing, although there are suspicions that it may have been as early as his teenage years. Even the exact number of his victims is still in doubt, although he did confess in gruesome detail to 30 homicides across seven states between the years of 1974 and 1978. The true total remains unknown and could be much higher.

What is known is that in 1974, Bundy entered the room of an 18-year-old university student, beat her with a metal rod and sexually assaulted her. She survived, just, but with permanent brain damage. Other students at other campuses were not so lucky, disappearing at the rate of about one per month over the next six months. Most of them disappeared at night, usually near ongoing construction work, and all within a week or so of exams. All of the victims were wearing jeans or other pants, and at most crime scenes there had been sightings of a man wearing a cast or a sling, and driving a brownish Volkswagen Beetle.

Police broadcast details of the killer, and a number of people from Bundy's university and his workplace stepped forward to identify Bundy as a possible match. However, police thought that it was unlikely that the squeaky-clean law student could be their killer.

At this time, Bundy was working for the Department of Emergency Services, where he first met and briefly dated a co-worker, Carole Ann Boone, a woman who'd already been married twice and had two children. Then Bundy moved to the University of Utah Law School in Salt Lake City, and the killings shifted too.

Computing was in its infancy then, but police ran all the available data on all the killings to date through a massive database. Out of thousands of names, 26 popped out – Ted Bundy among them. But it wasn't until 1976 that prosecutors finally gathered enough proof to charge him with murder.

You'd think that with the monster finally behind bars, police would do everything in their power to keep him there. However, on two separate occasions, Bundy managed the seemingly impossible – once by escaping from the courthouse; once by breaking into the ceiling crawl space of the prison in which he was being held. The second time he remained at large for some weeks, during which time he carried out a number of solo attacks and a 15-minute bloody rampage through a Florida sorority house that left two women dead and another two severely injured.

Bundy was finally caught when the car he was driving – another Beetle – was recognised by a police officer as being stolen. Inside were a number of stolen credit cards and one of the disguises he'd worn at the scene of an earlier murder. That was more than enough for police to re-examine what the honours student had really been up to over recent months.

Bundy was tried for the murders of the sorority girls, Lisa Levy and Martha Bowman, and sentenced to death, and it was during his next trial in Orlando – for the murder of a 12-year-old girl – that he married Carole Ann Boone, his former colleague. (She'd moved to Florida to be closer to Bundy in prison, and had visited him regularly.)

Their wedding ceremony was almost as unbelievable as the fact that anyone was actually prepared to marry such a depraved human being. Bundy, drawing on his legal background, took advantage of a loop-hole in Florida law proclaiming that any declaration of marriage in a courthouse in the presence of court officers is valid and legally binding.

Throughout the trial, Bundy had been acting as part of his own defence team, right down to questioning people on the stand. So no-one thought anything unusual was about to happen when he took over for the re-direct of his girlfriend, Carole Ann. Then he proposed.

According to the arcane law, the couple was now legally wed. But instead of a honeymoon, a wedding feast or any of the other normal trappings of marriage, a few short hours later, Bundy was sentenced to death for the third time and sent to Raiford Prison.

Boone stuck by her killer husband through thick and thin, even becoming pregnant to Bundy, or so she claimed, despite a lack of official conjugal visits between the two. Their daughter – or *a* daughter in any case – was born in October 1982.

Despite being sentenced to death three times, the execution wasn't going to happen any time soon. First there was the tortuous appeal process – with an increasingly more bizarrely behaved Bundy often representing himself – and a number of last-minute stays of execution, including one just a mere 15 minutes before he was scheduled to die on 2 July 1986, and another on 18 November, just seven hours before the big moment.

If his horrendous crimes hadn't been enough to put her off, the lengthy justice process finally proved too much for Carole Ann, who divorced Bundy and fled the state of Florida with her infant daughter.

On 17 January 1989, Bundy's final death warrant was issued, with the date set for just one week later. Bundy spent his last week in a marathon of confessions, sharing openly for the first time exactly how his 30 victims had met their ends. Bundy and his lawyers tried to delay the final sentence further by asking for more time for a fuller confession, but all of the families refused.

Bundy spoke to his mother, turned down the chance for a final meal, and was executed in the electric chair early in the morning of 24 January 1989. Somewhere in America, his ex-wife and daughter doubtless watched his death make headline news that night.

The Lonely Hearts Killer

Rodney Francis Cameron certainly had a rough start to life – his father died not long after he was born, and then he witnessed his mother dropping dead from a heart attack as she took a cake from the oven in the family kitchen. He was only seven years old.

The family who adopted him, doubtless hoping to give him a happier future, had little idea what kind of small monster they'd taken into their home. He was violent towards his classmates at school and constantly in trouble. At 10, he was found trying to strangle a young girl. A girlfriend during his teenage years went through the same ordeal. But the last straw for his adoptive family came when he was found trying to throttle an elderly woman in the street. By his late teens he was out on his own and spiralling into a life of alcohol, hallucinogenic drugs and Satanism. It was at this time he met and married his first wife, Brenda, an older woman who already had a young child of her own and had found something loveable about the troubled young man.

Cameron picked up work at a nursing home in the Blue Mountains, west of Sydney, and was befriended by one of the older nurses, Florence Jackson, who regularly welcomed him into her home and went out of her way to show him some kindness. He repaid her efforts by strangling her until she was unconscious, raping her and then finishing her off by stuffing a towel down her throat. It was a 'killer move' that he would soon repeat.

A week later, heading south to Melbourne, he hitched a lift with a 19-year-old bank clerk, Francesco Ciliberto, whom he bashed half to death with a rock then strangled with a football sock. Like the first victim, Francesco Ciliberto's body – when recovered from the bottom of a cliff where Cameron had thrown it – was found with a shirt stuffed down the throat.

After murdering the man who'd been kind enough to offer him a lift, Cameron stole his car and headed for Queensland. There, on 21 February 1974, he was captured after kidnapping a mother and daughter. On his arrest, he explained his actions to police saying that he 'had to kill three'. Given that by now he'd already killed twice, both mother and daughter were lucky to be rescued in time. He was sentenced to prison for life for the two earlier murders.

While incarcerated, a lifelong friend, a nurse named Anne, got back in touch. Whether she was motivated by sheer kindness or his newfound notoriety, isn't known. It's hard to believe that she'd been holding a torch for him since his troubled teenage years, when he tried to strangle his girlfriend of the time. But Anne fell in love. Cameron at the time was still married to Brenda, so needed to divorce her before marrying Anne.

Safely behind bars, it seemed unlikely that the two could ever do more than hold hands in a prison waiting room; however, an appeal against the length of his sentence had surprising results.

On the 12 March 1990, after serving 16 years in prison, the decision was made that Cameron was 'fully rehabilitated' and no longer a threat to society. Anne and her 38-year-old husband were soon free to begin their life together.

Little did Anne suspect that while they were finally settling into 'normal' married life – their interaction no longer taking place in a waiting room under the watchful eyes of prison officials and fellow prisoners – Cameron was already hunting his next victim, using a late-night radio matchmaking program on Melbourne's 3AW to search for a partner 'willing to share his happiness'. Six women responded to his description of himself as a non-drinking, non-smoking marine biologist and Gemini. One of these women, 44-year old Maria Goellner, was unlucky enough to make a date with him.

A few weeks later, Maria was found lying dead on a motel-room floor in the Blue Mountains, the same area where Cameron had committed his first murder 16 years earlier. She too had something stuffed down her throat – a handkerchief in this case. The body was strewn with carnations. Also alongside the body was a note to his wife, reading in part: 'Anne, I am sorry. Had I not done what happened, my life would have been destroyed. Love eternally, Rodney'. A week later, he gave himself up to police at Deniliquin in New South Wales. At his trial, Cameron was jailed again for life, and this time his file was marked 'never to be released'.

But there was another gruesome detail still to emerge. While in jail, the Lonely Hearts Killer asked to speak to police. During that interview, he confessed to the murder of another woman – 79-year-old Sarah McKenzie – whose death he'd been suspected of at one time, but for which he'd never been prosecuted. While it was known that she had been stabbed 30 times and then bludgeoned with a mattock, his confession included precise details that only the killer could have known, and that had never been made public. Case solved.

Later still, so too were four more murders. In an interview with the crime reporter from the Sydney *Herald Sun*, Cameron also confessed to the murders of two other women in Victoria in 1990, both victims of frenzied knife attacks, the bashing death of a man in South Australia in 1974, and the strangulation of a woman in New South Wales, also in 1974. These were cold cases, long unsolved, but it's still unknown whether he really did carry them out, or whether he was just trying to make his way onto the list of Australia's worst serial killers.

Second Time Unlucky

Prison librarian, 23-year old Helen Cusack, paid the greatest price for falling in love with an inmate at the Junee Correctional Centre, 45 kilometres south of Sydney's CBD. David Barac was in jail for stabbing his first wife – in fact, stabbing her so hard that the knife blade broke from the handle – yet Helen found something loveable about the 28-year-old Peruvian-born chef. He was parolled in February 1995, and she married him immediately.

Two months later, she was dead.

David Barac's first wife, Joanne, had been somewhat luckier . . . if being critically wounded rather than killed can be considered lucky at all. After a violent and tumultuous marriage, she finally left him in 1992, only to find herself on the business end of a knife wielded by her outraged, soon-to-be ex-husband.

At the trial, David Barac presented himself as completely contrite for his loss of control and was sentenced to a bare two-year jail sentence. It was during his time inside the Junee Correctional Centre that he met Helen.

Notwithstanding Barac's past history, Helen clearly believed that his violence towards the very person he'd promised to love and honour had been a momentary lapse of judgement . . . a one-off. Obviously gambling on this fact, she married him, but the cracks began to show immediately.

The man she'd met in the library of the prison wasn't the man with whom she was now sharing her life. Or perhaps it was the same man, but his mask had finally slipped. Of course, on the outside, Barac now had access to drugs and alcohol. He confessed to a long history of cocaine, cannabis and tranquiliser abuse dating back to his teenage years at school, moving onto heroin and acid when he lived in Israel in the 1980s.

Just like Barac's first wife, Helen demanded a separation, however, she clearly trusted Barac enough to agree to meet him when he told her that he was about to be deported and had to face a hearing in Canberra.

In a show of support, in April 1995, just after the newlyweds had separated, Helen ironed a shirt for him, hung his good grey suit in her car, and set off for a rendezvous point in Canberra. She was never seen alive again.

Barac's first story to his friends was that they'd met up and talked, gone to a motel, and then had a fight about her family – how they were poisoning her mind against him and didn't want the newlyweds to be together. He'd stormed out and then driven her car back to Sydney. He explained away some cuts on his hand as injuries from a beer bottle. To other friends, he confessed what he had really done, but they sent him away and told him that they didn't want to know.

In the very early morning a couple of days later, Barac turned up at the Ashfield Police Station, arriving in Helen Cusack's car. His story was rambling, and police were worried enough to send him to hospital, but throughout it all, Barac still claimed that he had no idea where his wife was. He was placed under arrest for breaching one of the conditions of his parole – namely, to stay away from alcohol – and was sent to the Correctional Centre at Maitland.

However, unbeknown to him, the cell was bugged, and detectives soon found themselves listening to a frank confession as to what had really happened to his wife.

In fact, when Barac had driven back to Sydney from Canberra, his wife's body was already in the boot of the car. During their argument, he'd stabbed her and shoved her in there. Then, noticing that she was still alive, he'd finished off the gruesome task. He'd later hidden her body at a site off the Pacific Highway, a few kilometres from Mooney Mooney, on the way to Newcastle.

On tape, Barac asked his cell mate whether he'd help move Helen's body to a better permanent site once the cell mate was released from jail. He even drew his cell mate a map of where the body was to be found. All this information was gold to the investigators listening in, and a search of the area described by Barac soon revealed his wife's body. The clothes that Helen had so carefully prepared for his 'deportation hearing' were discovered a few metres away, covered in blood. A forensic examination of her car uncovered traces of her blood in the boot and interior of the car, as well as hairs in the well for the spare tyre and on the rear parcel shelf.

At his trial, Barac pleaded guilty to murder. He was given the maximum sentence of life imprisonment; during sentencing, the Crown took into consideration both Barac's attack upon his former wife, and the fact that he'd clearly planned the murder in advance. Not only had he lured Helen to meet him in Canberra on the pretext of a phony deportation hearing, but he'd also gone along armed with a knife that he'd taken from the house he was sharing in Rozelle.

David Barac was sentenced to 30 years in prison, with a non-parole period of 20 years. His comment at the time: 'Sometimes, I don't know how to love'.

The earliest date for Barac's release is 25 May 2017, when he will be 61 years of age. You'd think that having grievously injured one wife and killed the second, no woman would be lining up for the role of Wife Number Three. However, in July 2006, the *Sydney Morning Herald* reported that yet another woman – known as Mercedes – was seen in the Supreme Court trying to overturn a three-year ban on her visits to David Barac.

Teen Love Rekindled

He was Bianca Roberts' first boyfriend, at age 11, and by the time they met again, nearly two decades later, James Vlassakis was one of Australia's most notorious killers, widely considered a monster, a serial killer and one of the deviants responsible for the Snowtown bodies-in-barrels murders.

Vlassakis, aged 29 at the time of his trial, pleaded guilty to four murders, including those of his half-brothers Troy Youde and David Johnson, as well as two other men, Gary O'Dwyer and Frederick Brooks. In fact, Vlassakis and his co-accused – murder-spree ringleader John Justin Bunting, Robert Joe Wagner and Mark Ray Haydon – are thought to be responsible for the murders of 11 people in South Australia between 1992 and 1999. Eight of the bodies were found dismembered in barrels of acid in a disused Snowtown bank vault on 20 May 1999.

Most of the bodies had been tortured, dismembered and stripped of their flesh by Bunting and Wagner, who used tools including handcuffs, pliers, sparklers and an electric shock machine.

The reason for their murders? All 11 had had the misfortune to cross paths with John Bunting, an odd little man who looked incapable of any harm, but who had a particular hatred for paedophiles, and would rant for hours about the horrible nature of what they did to children and how they should be stopped. Bunting detested homosexuals and drug users with almost equal passion.

It was an accident of location that first brought the killing gang together. Bunting lived in Salisbury North, in Adelaide's northern suburbs. So too did Robert Joe Wagner, and his partner Barry Lane – a transsexual who was also known as Vanessa. Bunting tolerated Lane at first as a source of information about homosexuals, but eventually Lane would end up on the gang's list of victims. The other member of the murder gang was Mark Ray Haydon (who used the pseudonym Mark Lawrence to rent the bank in Snowtown), a quiet man who was obsessed with cars and who'd met Bunting at a TAFE welding course. (Haydon's wife was also to become one of Bunting's victims.)

The final member of the murder gang was James Vlassakis, known as Jamie, who first came into Bunting's orbit when Bunting began a relationship with Jamie's mother, Elizabeth Harvey. At this stage, Harvey was divorced and mother to four sons – James, Adrian, Kristoffer and Troy. She had a long history of abuse, a big gambling problem, and a blind spot when it came to falling in love with men who would do her harm.

By the time she moved in with Bunting to the house in 203 Waterloo Corner Road, Bunting had already killed twice. The body of a young gay man, Clinton Tresize, had been buried in a farmer's field near the hamlet of Lower Light by the Gulf of St Vincent in South Australia. Ray Davies, a man whom Bunting believed was a child abuser, was actually buried in the yard of 203 Waterloo Corner Road, out the back near the water tank.

Davies' body was later to be joined by that of Suzanne Allen, Davies' ex-partner. In a bizarre twist of fate, Allen herself had fallen for Bunting, and when he became tired of her mooning around after him, he got rid of her in a very final manner. (Her body was later uncovered in the yard of Waterloo Corner Road, chopped into bits and buried in 11 separate plastic bags.)

And this is the house where the young Jamie lived with his

mother and his 'father figure', Bunting. Jamie had already had a rough start in life – he was abused by his biological father first, then his half-brother, Troy Youde, and then a neighbour across the road at a previous address. He'd also watched his father die from a heart attack when he was just seven years old. With his troubled past and history of abuse, Jamie was easy prey for the manipulative Bunting, who was on a mission to rid the world of abusers and homosexuals.

In 1997, Bunting and the gang began to put their plan into action, first killing a young gay man who was boarding with them, and then Wagner's ex-partner, Barry Lane. Over the next two years, the body count continued to grow. It ended when police entered the old bank vault in Snowtown and found the bodies of eight people, squashed into six barrels of hydrochloric acid. Bunting, Wagner and Haydon were arrested the next day; Jamie gave himself up to police a week later.

The discovery of the bodies, the arrest of the killers and their trial provoked a media storm, and that's when Bianca Roberts first heard what her childhood boyfriend had been up to. She began to write to Jamie in prison.

At his trial, Vlassakis pleaded guilty to four of the murders and was jailed for life, with a non-parole period of 26 years. He became the star witness against his erstwhile mentor, John Justin Bunting, as well as Robert Joe Wagner, both of whom were later sentenced to automatic life terms for each of the murders.

When asked whether they had anything to say, Bunting remained silent but Wagner read out prepared statement: 'Paedophiles were doing terrible things to children and innocent children were being damaged. The authorities did nothing about it. I was very angry. Somebody had to do something about it. I decided to take action. I took that action'.

The final one to be sentenced was Mark Ray Haydon, who

had been convicted of five counts of assisting offenders over his involvement in the disposal of bodies at the Snowtown bank. He was sentenced to 25 years' jail with 18 years' non-parole.

Jamie had already begun his prison sentence, and within six months the friendly letters from his childhood girlfriend had turned to romance. In an interview in 2009, Bianca Roberts told *That's Life* magazine that she planned to marry Vlassakis. She said that he still had the same 'stop-you-in-your-tracks eyes and smile' as he had as an innocent 11 year old.

She explained that although others saw him as a serial killer, she loved him and chose not to view him that way. She blamed his involvement in the crimes on the 'brainwashing' he'd received from Bunting, and said that while she wished they could be together like a normal couple, she couldn't help loving whom she loved, and that she was prepared to wait for James – even until 2025, when he will first become eligible for parole.

The news that the serial killer might be getting married – in the grim setting of Yatala, one of Australia's toughest jails – caused another media storm. However, the Correctional Services Minister of the time, Tom Koutsantonis, told Parliament that, 'It won't be happening on my watch'. Bianca Roberts has since disappeared from media view.

Chapter 6
The Longest Stretch

Gemma and Greg Walsh look at each other like any married couple who can still count the number of nights they have spent together as man and wife. The difference is that they have now been married for six years – she lives in a pretty town somewhere in regional Australia; he lives behind bars in a medium-security prison about 20 kilometres away. Gemma lives on a disability pension after an accident at work. Walsh is doing life for the rape and murder of a young female neighbour – a crime he committed around 25 years ago, long before he and Gemma began their relationship or thought of marriage. Theirs is not your typical love story – a convicted rapist and murderer hardly being your typical Mr Right – but it is definitely a love story.

Day by Day

Gemma's car could probably navigate its way to the prison quite successfully by itself, given that she estimates she has made the trek around 1000 times in the past five years – three and sometimes four times a week without fail, usually on Friday, Saturday and Sunday afternoons. It's a beautiful drive too, heading out of town past a lake and rolling farmland to the prison itself. From the main road, there's not much to see – an unobtrusive sign, and a dusty lane leading to the visitors' car park. A small brick shed on the edge of the car park houses a simple wooden bench and lockers for those who don't want to leave their belongings in their car while they visit, but as Gemma wryly says: 'I don't know what they're worried about. All the bad guys are locked up inside, aren't they?'

Gemma's routine rarely alters. She grabs a lighter and a couple of cigarettes from an open packet, stashes her mobile phone in the car, and places her driver's licence, an unopened packet of cigarettes and $10 in coins into a clear plastic bag. She knows that after she has buzzed the gate, she'll have just enough time to smoke the two loose cigarettes before the prison staff come down to let her in. The lighter isn't allowed to be taken into the prison, so she stashes it on top of the lockers. It hasn't been nicked while she has been inside the prison – or at least, not yet. The money is for Walsh, who is allowed to receive $10 from each of his visitors. The unopened cigarettes, a prison rule to ensure that nothing illicit is being smuggled in, are for Walsh and Gemma during the visit.

There are almost 200 men living inside this facility, but generally there are only a handful of visitors at any particular time, including some young mothers bringing babies and toddlers to visit their dads for a few brief hours of quality time, albeit under the eyes of the prison officers. Gemma knows many of the regulars by sight, if not by name, and as they chat around the gate waiting to be let in, gallows humour rules. Most of the officers are friendly, but there are a couple of bastards – male and female – and all the visitors hope that the nasty ones are not on duty. It can mean all the difference between a relaxed visit, and one filled with tension – a visit where she can hold hands and kiss her husband, and one where they have to sit apart.

Gemma likes to be first in the queue – mainly so she has as much time as possible with Walsh, but also so she can snaffle a table equipped with more comfortable chairs – she's often in pain from her accident at work.

Generally the tables at the front of the room – closer to the officers – are reserved for prisoners who are considered a higher security risk than Walsh. Prisoners with a High 2 security rating are only allowed one-hour visits – rather than the three hours afforded to low-security prisoners – and while High 2 prisoners are in the visiting room, the door to the outdoor courtyard is kept locked. By the time that one hour is up, Gemma is usually gasping to get outside for a cigarette. So, too, are some of the officers.

'When the officers come down to let us into the prison, they look just like something out of *Homicide* or *Division 4* or another cop show, with their uniforms and mirrored sunnies', says Gemma. 'One of these days, we are all going to start humming the theme song.'

Visitors are let into the prison in small groups, and escorted through what is essentially a no-man's land between the front gate and a second gate leading into a guardhouse. High wire fences, topped with rolls of razor wire, surround the whole place. This may not be a high-security facility, but they still don't want anyone escaping.

Inside the guardhouse, visitors empty their pockets into a plastic basket then step through a metal detector similar to those found at airports. Even though Gemma has been a regular visitor to this prison for five years, her ID is still carefully scrutinised. 'They'll say, "Gidday Gemma, here to see Greg? How are you going? Where's your licence?"'

Security formalities over, another gate is opened and then the visitors walk down a concrete path through manicured gardens to the visiting room. It's not surprising that the gardens are immaculately maintained. The lawns, and the beds of roses, daisies and rockery plants are looked after by the inmates, all of whom have plenty of time on their hands and little to fill it.

As always, Walsh is waiting anxiously to see Gemma. He peers through the window for a first glimpse of his wife. A tall man with a shaved head and neatly trimmed moustache, he is an imposing sight thanks to hours spent in the prison gym over the years. At least in the beginning, the body-building was a form of self-defence. 'They always pick on the new ones, and because of the crime I committed, I was definitely a target', he explains. When he was first arrested, Walsh was beaten severely by another inmate. The white scar across the back of his head is a lasting memento, but today – with his powerful arms and legs, not to mention his years of experience in picking his way through the politics of prison – it's doubtful that anyone would be foolish enough to take him on. He is a lifer, an old-timer, and he knows his way around.

The middle-aged man who is waiting so eagerly to see Gemma this weekend is a very different person from the young man who was described by the judge at his original trial as 'a figure of nightmare'.

One thing that is not in doubt in Walsh's guilt – he never denied his actions, only his intent to kill. Likewise, his remorse is evident. 'In one day, I destroyed so many lives – not only that of Louisa, but also her family and friends. They have to live with what I did every day . . . just like I do. There are no words to describe how sorry I am.'

Every night, Walsh says a prayer for the young woman whose life he took. For a while, his psychologist advised him to stop – thinking that Walsh was becoming obsessive over his guilt – but Walsh has since returned to his nightly ritual. 'I have to do it. I have to believe that there is something after life for her, and that my prayers today might help.'

For years now, Gemma also has to live with the consequences of Walsh's actions. She knew about the case before they were a couple, and describes it very simply. 'Greg broke into a neighbour's house to get money when he was drunk. He found a girl there, raped her and during the rape, she died.'

For those who wonder how a woman could fall in love with a man who has committed a crime like Walsh's, Gemma has this to say:

Everyone is innocent in jail, but Greg has always admitted his guilt. I live with it every day too. I think of the girl, Louisa, although I never knew her, but I feel for her and for her family. People say to me, 'You have daughters, how can you . . .?' And if something happened to my daughters, I'd feel much the same way as Louisa's family do. But I know Greg, and I know he is so full of remorse. He is a man who made one horrible mistake – he is not a psychopath. And people should be given the chance to change and redeem themselves.

The 20-year old girl had recently moved out of home into a place of her own and should have had her whole life ahead of her. Instead, she was unfortunate enough to be at home when Walsh, in a very drunken state, broke into her apartment.

Walsh pleaded guilty to the charges of unlawful assault with carnal knowledge, unlawful entry and stealing. He pleaded not guilty to the charge of murder, however following trial by jury, Walsh was found guilty of the murder too. He was sentenced to life imprisonment for the murder, 10 years' imprisonment for the assault, four years' imprisonment for the unlawful entry, and one year's imprisonment for the stealing. At the time of sentencing, Walsh's sentence was taken to include a non-parole period of 20 years.

Today Walsh says, 'I had never done anything like that before. Plenty of times I'd drunk the same amount with no effect, but this time it affected me differently. I can only describe it as going troppo, although I know that is no excuse for what I did.'

An Education in Life

Greg Walsh never knew his biological parents, and one wonders whether either of them know that the baby they gave up for adoption in the 1950s in the UK is nearing his 25th year of imprisonment on the other side of the world. It's not something that Walsh likes to think about, but one day he would like to make contact. He has gone so far as to trace his original birth certificate, which has his birth mother's name. The rest will have to wait until he is out of jail.

Adopted shortly after his birth, Walsh migrated to Australia with his new parents. His was not a happy childhood – he found school difficult and boring, and by the time he was 15, he left education behind for good. Or that was the plan.

Being locked up in prison year after year can make what seemed boring to a lively teenager somewhat more attractive to an adult. While in his first prison, Walsh took courses in everything from painting to algebra, and even accident action.

But of far more importance to Walsh was the education he received on himself. 'I've done every course I could – victim awareness, anger management, assertiveness skills, sexual offending treatment, domestic violence for men, how to prevent a relapse with drugs and alcohol . . . I don't want to ever have a reason to end up back in here again.'

Drugs and alcohol had been an issue for Walsh since his teens – he started with cannabis when he was just 15, and then began drinking heavily from 17. It was an explosive mixture, and Walsh was constantly in fights – and occasionally in detox centres. Somehow though he managed to hold down a succession of jobs – as a labourer, a printer, a painter, building wheelchairs and working in factories. He was considered reliable, dependable and hard working. But one day, while drunk, he committed a robbery and was caught. He fled his home state and drifted north, ending up in a rented house where his path was to fatally cross that of Louisa.

'While in my first prison, I saw a psychologist for years, which really helped me understand my behaviour', says Walsh. 'I was a very angry person when I first went to prison, but the psychologist helped me get a handle on that. He has since become a very good friend and supporter.'

Gemma agrees: 'All the reports say that Greg has rehabilitated himself beautifully. He's done every course available. At home, I have all of his certificates – 12 boxes of stuff I have collected since we've been together.'

Indeed, in one of the many court reports Gemma has tucked away, the judge noted in his conclusions:

> On the subjective side the information before the court shows that [Mr Walsh] has worked hard at attempting to reform himself while he has been in prison. He has been allowed into the community on conditional licence for extended periods and he has demonstrated that the prospects of him being successfully re-integrated into the community are good. [Mr Walsh] admits that he is responsible for the crimes that he committed and he is remorseful for his crimes. He is cognitively and effectively able to express empathy towards his victim and the risk of his re-offending has been significantly reduced.

Knowing her husband as well as she does, Gemma too thinks that there is little chance of Walsh re-offending.

> I've also done my own research and found out that the recidivism rate for rape and murder is like a fraction of a per cent whereas for the druggies or drink drivers is much, much higher. Recidivism rates are much lower for those who've spent more than 12 years in jail, because they just do not want to go back there again.

Today, Walsh doesn't even touch fizzy drinks, preferring plain, cold rainwater. 'My darling used to drink six or 10 cans of soft drink during a visit, but no longer. He'll have a couple of chocolates and some chips and that will be it', says Gemma.

Even his aftershave has to be alcohol free, Walsh insists. In one of his many daily phone calls with Gemma, they debate where she might be able to get hold of some, and the merits of shaving balm versus aftershave: 'And I'm not having any of that moisturiser crap!' Walsh insists. It's the normal kind of conversation you'd hear between a husband and wife, notable only for the fact that Walsh knows that alcohol is something that he needs to stay away from for the rest of his life – even the small amount in an innocuous container of aftershave.

As for drugs, staying away from them in prison is not as easy as you'd think, says Gemma.

When he was younger, Greg used to do pot, but no hard drugs. I'm really proud that he has stayed away from it, because in jail, you can find pot right, left and centre. They can get hold of everything they need in there. Blind Freddy can see who's passing it, but nothing is ever done about it.

Love at Third Sight

Gemma and Walsh first met briefly in Sydney in the mid-1980s through a mutual friend – someone from Gemma's hometown in regional New South Wales. She'd grown up on a property there – horses, boarding school, the whole rural deal. Then she'd headed to the big smoke where she worked in bars and had fun, lots of fun.

Her brother's life wasn't quite so carefree – he'd become involved in drugs and spent time in prison. Gemma used to visit him there, so although she's never had so much as a parking ticket herself, as the saying goes, she wasn't fazed by the idea of visiting someone in prison. That's a definite advantage for someone who ends up marrying a lifer.

Fast-forward to the year 2000, and while Sydney was in full party mode for the Olympics, Gemma was living in a mining town, with one divorce behind her, and her second husband recently deceased. Her kids were off on their own by then, so when a letter arrived from Walsh, it took little to convince her to take a brief holiday.

'In prison, Greg had been making beautiful leather products and other craftworks. He wanted some gems to decorate them, and a friend suggested he write to me. I'd been buying and selling gems, so I offered to come up for a visit and bring some for him.'

Gemma stayed 14 days that first trip, but Walsh says that by the third time they met, he knew that there was something between them. Gemma was smitten too. 'Over the next while I flew up and back a few times, then I decided that I wouldn't mind going up there for six months and having a taste of the summer. Those six months turned into 12 months, and then more . . . And now look at us – it's been 13 years!'

Her experience visiting Walsh in prison turned the forthright country girl into a prison-reform crusader.

The prison was the most horrific place to be. Up there, the prisoners were mainly blacks and they were treated shockingly. The families would drive 800 kilometres to visit their son or husband or whatever. They'd be 10 minutes late because the river had been up or something, and the guards would simply tell them to fuck off. Oooh, yes, the blacks get treated very differently.

Gemma joined forces with a number of other prison families and fought hard for some simple reforms.

Even little things like getting the phone calls extended. We managed to get details on how many minutes prisoners in every other jail in Australia got. We used to ring up other jails and pretend that we were university students doing research and then they'd tell us anything we asked about.

Gemma says that the prison did eventually allow the prisoners more time on the phone than 10 minutes – one minute more. Still, it was a start.

We made that many appointments to try and see the Minister, and talk about what was happening, but it was pointless. We were trouble and the Minister would cross the street if we were spotted. But we did get to know some of the departmental staff quite well. One of the other wives and I were there at the department so often that we used to sign in under all sorts of different names – Fred and Wilma, Ditzy and Fuzzy, Bugs Bunny and Elmer. They knew us so we'd just waltz in and sign in under any name. One day, in 20 years' time, someone is going to notice that Fred Flintstone signed in and out for the day.

Prison food was another issue on which they campaigned hard.

It was shocking. On Fridays, they'd get one tiny piece of fish and a few veggies. Other days, they'd make up a stew and for the rest of the week they'd just curry it and curry it until it was gone. The inmates were allowed one piece of fruit per week. I'd like to see how the fat dietician they had would have survived on that!

Prisoners in the low-security section – which was separate from the main jail – fared even worse with prison fare, Gemma says.

They'd push the trolley with food up from the main jail then someone from low security would have to be sent to collect it.

Sometimes it would be left at the gate for hours at a time – in the heat and humidity or pissing down rain. The salads would go soggy, the hot stuff would go cold . . . it's a wonder no one died of food poisoning. Most of the time, Greg just had to throw the food straight in the bin. Greg and practically everyone else in that prison lived on three-minute noodles. You wouldn't believe the dishes he can cook up from them – casseroles, stir fries . . . they pretty much kept him alive in that prison because the food they provided was so bad.

One of Gemma's lowest points – one of the few times she has cried while Walsh has been inside – came on one Christmas Day when she received a phone call from Walsh, who told her that they'd been given dinner but no knives or forks. One of the prisoners had asked a guard for cutlery and had been told: 'Eat it with your fucking fingers. You're no more than an animal anyway'.

After a letter to the editor in the local paper from one former prisoner, one of the senior staff from the department – who knew Gemma from her campaigning – rang her and asked if the food was as bad as all that. He asked her to keep a diary of the food Walsh received over the course of a week, and his response when he saw it was: 'My teenage boy would eat more than that in a day!'

The Bottom Line

Now transferred interstate to another prison, Walsh works four days out of seven in the garden, for which he gets paid $28.60 or approximately $7 a day. He estimates that by the time his 25 years are up, he'll have earned about $400 in superannuation.

For daily expenses – aftershave, snacks – much of the time, he's dependent on the coins that Gemma can bring in the plastic bag on each visit. Money orders can also be sent but these cost about $8 each – hardly worth it if you can only afford to send $20 in total.

It's not something the administration probably considered when they introduced the money-order system so that they didn't have to handle cash.

For Gemma, even coming up with a handful of coins is a constant struggle. Since 2008, she has been on a disability pension following a fall on a slippery floor at work that broke some vertebrae in her neck. 'There was nothing I could do about it – my feet just went out from under me and I went head over heels.'

Walsh was on the phone to Gemma at the time and describes this as one of the most frightening moments of his imprisonment. 'I was completely powerless. I knew something had happened and was yelling down the phone for them to call an ambulance, to do something to help Gemma. But I couldn't tell if they could hear me, and I had no idea what was happening.'

Today, Gemma survives on $340 a fortnight after regular deductions for bills such as her car and contents insurance. Out of this she pays all Walsh's living expenses too. There is always welfare, but Gemma loathes the idea of a handout. 'I've only been to welfare three times in five years because I hate going there. I'll live on a loaf of bread for a week if I have to.'

Even though Gemma and Walsh are married, she only gets paid the single pension – because the state is 'taking care of Greg'. But it's the unexpected expenses that are the killer.

'When digital TV came in, if we wanted to be able to watch it, we were told we had to buy a special TV that had been made in prison somewhere. The TVs were all see-though, so you couldn't hide anything inside, and they cost $300', explains Walsh.

Gemma somehow scraped together the money, only for the prison officers to change their mind and supply all prisoners with a regular TV – for which they were expected to pay a weekly rental. 'Being made to buy the other TV was a complete waste of money – and that was money we didn't have. I've still got their silly little prison TV at home somewhere', says Gemma. Maybe it will be a collectible one day . . .

For the families of most prisoners, finances are a major issue, says Gemma. 'When I'm visiting Greg, I'll see women out there with three little kiddies and then you see the wife handing over money to the husband and I think, "I wonder what are the rest of you going to eat for the rest of the week?"'

Health is also a constant problem, with prisoners being allocated only a certain amount of funding each year for necessities such as dental care. Like many prisoners, Walsh is now missing a couple of teeth – removal being far cheaper than repair – and some others could do with some serious attention, but he's limited to only a few hundreds of dollars of dental care each year. 'I can't stand it when he has toothache – if he's in pain, I'm in pain too', says Gemma. But there is nothing more they can do while he is still inside. And at least he has some teeth left. One of his fellow prisoners is now down to his bare gums.

The situation with their legal bills is similar. Funding legal action – particularly in a case as convoluted as Walsh's – would not be possible without the help of legal aid or the kindness of lawyers who've taken a particular interest in the human rights implications of his case.

'I've nothing but praise for the people who have helped me', says Walsh. 'I'm not complaining about doing time – I really do believe that if you do the crime, you should serve the time – but it is very difficult when the goal posts keep changing. It is hard to keep up hope.'

Another Door Slams Shut

Walsh was transferred interstate not long before his 20-year non-parole period was up. His father was terminally ill (his mother had died in the 1980s), and he was allowed the transfer on compassionate grounds. Gemma followed the path of his plane in a four-wheel drive with all her possessions. She moved in with Walsh's father, Adrian, and was Adrian's carer until he passed away. Inheriting Adrian's furniture was a boon – Walsh will have something familiar when he comes out of prison. Besides, Gemma can't afford new furniture on a disability pension. Walsh will also recognise the boxes of certificates and paperwork Gemma has accumulated over the past 13 years, the samples of his leatherwork, and a few of his drawings – exquisite sketches of budgies and other artworks line the walls of Gemma's current living room. He's never seen this room though – he's still waiting for the chance for day release again.

For a while, though, everything was looking promising for Walsh. He was back in his hometown – albeit in prison. He was close to his father at a critical time. Gemma was looking after his father. And his 20-year non-parole period was almost over. The end was in sight.

Preparations for Walsh's release began, but first came his marriage to Gemma. They'd planned on getting married two years earlier, but at the last minute, permission had been cancelled.

> We'd been going to get married in 2004. His father was going to fly in, and the prison officials had said that there wouldn't be a problem. They said that we could get married at home, that they'd send two officers, then at the last minute they pulled the pin.

In the end, they were able to tie the knot in 2006.

> An officer drove Greg down from prison to his father's house, and we got married there with just a few witnesses, including the chaplain from his previous prison and a friend from the Salvation Army. The officer actually ended up videotaping the

wedding for us, and even volunteered to watch my father in law while we went and . . . well, did what newly married couples do. It was wonderful. We had about eight hours together that day, then they took Greg home to prison.

In their vows, Walsh promised: 'I bring my commitment to my relationship with Gemma. I bring my love and care for her and my hope for a positive future'. Gemma in turn promised: 'I bring my love for Greg. I bring my strength of character, my steadiness and my hope for a positive future'.

At the time, their hopes for a positive future were looking good.

As part of his release preparation, Walsh was found a temporary job, for which he was allowed to leave prison each day. Gemma still remembers him calling her one day after a trip to a petrol station with his boss. 'Greg had been allowed to go inside and buy himself a packet of chips and a Coke. He couldn't believe how much they cost, it had been so long since he'd bought anything!'

As well as being allowed home to his father's house on short visits – at first in the company of two prison officers for two hours, then with one officer for four or six hours at a stretch – Walsh also found himself a more permanent job with a building crew who had employed former criminals before. 'The guys there were great, and didn't mind the fact that I'd been in prison.'

As the months went on, the couple slowly started to re-establish themselves financially. Walsh's boss was happy with his work and he was earning quite well. They even managed to save some money for their future. Walsh was allowed to catch the train by himself into town to do a class, or to get a lift with his boss to get to work. Meanwhile, Gemma was happy at home looking after Walsh's father.

The one thing that pissed me off was a young woman who was a parole officer. Even though Greg had passed the Sexual Behaviour Course with flying colours, she had the cheek to ring me up and say that she was worried about my safety. I said, 'Are you for fucking real? What happened was 20 years ago! If you're going to be worried about someone's safety, I'd be more worried about his!'

Gemma isn't joking. She's adamant that the man she married is no risk to society at all these days.

Then came the news that Walsh's original sentence was being extended by another five years. From minimum security, relative freedom, a job, a new wife and a lot of hope for the future, suddenly he was whisked back to maximum security.

A Secret Life

Today, Walsh is nearing the end of 25 years in prison and has been moved to yet another prison. Gemma has moved again to be near him, but not many people know her whole story. 'People ask me who my husband is, and I just say that he works at the prison. It's true. He does work there – he works in the garden and he does get paid for it.'

Every day, Gemma treads a fine line. 'But telling people that my husband works at the prison makes them clam up. The screws hate the cops, the cops hate the screws, and everyone hates the prisoners. It's all politics.'

As for the other prisoners – the men with whom Walsh has lived for so many years – Gemma says that she doesn't presume to judge other people. 'I don't judge anyone on anything. They are in there and doing their time. I'm not God and I am not a judge. Once they are doing their time, that should be it. Besides, there are a lot around town who should be in there too! They just haven't been caught yet.'

She's not close to many of the other jail families. 'There are probably only about three people I'd have back to my house.'

Of the people who find out that Walsh is actually a prisoner, Gemma says that 90 per cent are very supportive and that about 10 per cent don't want to know her. In the days when she was still working, Walsh's story was featured in the local newspaper.

Our lawyer had wanted to show how Greg had changed over time, how he'd softened and learned, so asked us if we'd be prepared to share the photos of our wedding with a journalist from the ABC. That was fine, but the next thing I knew, I was sitting in the staff room at work, flicking through the local paper and there was my wedding photo.

Gemma explained the situation to her boss, who was very supportive and agreed to let her have a couple of days off until the news had died down. 'She told me to go home straight away, and that she'd remove the page from the paper in the staff room so no one else would see it.' Three days later Gemma returned to work, only to be greeted by one of her regular customers. 'He grabbed my hand and told me that it was all going to be all right . . . that people wouldn't remember in a week, and that he didn't care who my husband was. All I could say was thank you. But it really meant a lot, for us not to be judged.'

Both Gemma and Walsh wish that the prison staff could be a little more understanding and non-judgemental too. Many of the people who run courses for prisoners are very young, which concerns Gemma. 'The real problem is that they have no experience of life. They've read a few textbooks, been to a few nightclubs and think they know it all. It pisses me off so much when people say that they are worried for my safety. Being with Greg is my choice.'

Gemma and Walsh have the same concerns about the prison staff as they do about those who run the rehabilitation programs. 'No experience at all most of them, although there are some young ones who've been around and know what they're doing.' And there is the one prison guard who told Gemma that he had been in the back of a paddy wagon many times himself over the years, and that it was only good fortune that meant he was on the right side of the bars. He is a good bloke, Gemma reckons, and one that the prisoners would probably respect. Not like some . . .

One guard is known as The Bastard because he is always standing at the window or door listening in on people's conversations. And there is one evil bitch who spends her time leaning out the door to check if anyone is smoking in their cell. Sure, they are not meant to smoke in there during the day, but who is going to hurt aside from themselves. Going hard on petty infringements while turning a blind eye to real issues like drugs in prison and the lack of rehabilitation is what makes the system so ridiculous.

Portents and Signs

Gemma is an Aquarian; Walsh a Virgo. Gemma says that leads to amusing differences in the way they approach life. 'It's a running joke between us that he'll ask me what the time is and I'll say, "sometime after three o'clock". But if you ask him, he'll say, "It's eight and a half minutes past three".'

'You can tell she's the kind of person who just goes with the flow', says Greg. 'Look at the way she'll just tip the Twisties and chips together – all on the same plate!' The one thing they do agree on is the importance of signs, portents and omens and other things that allow them some hope.

I got our astrology charts done for one of Greg's appeals and I told his lawyer that the stars said we were going to win it. The lawyer laughed and said that he wished he had my confidence. He gave us only about an 8 per cent chance of even getting a hearing.

But Gemma is an eternal optimist and a firm believer in the stars, so she wasn't too surprised when the lawyer said that they'd been given a hearing. They later won that appeal, although Walsh's release was still to prove problematic.

Allowed to be with his father when he was dying, Walsh says he asked him to send a sign from the other side if he possibly could. He'd like to know that there is a better place waiting for people like Louisa. And even today he's cheered by the fact that one day, years ago, when sitting alone in his cell with the door and window closed and no possibility of a draught, suddenly the curtains started flapping by themselves. 'That was definitely a sign from my father, I reckon. There was no other explanation for how they started moving.'

Walsh has also had the eerie experience of hearing a voice calling out to him one day as he was heading to a prison roll call, or muster. The other prisoners told him that they had heard nothing, and to this day, Greg reckons that voice calling his name was a message from his mother, who'd passed away some time before. Now he has his hopes pinned on what the strange behaviour of a little willy wagtail might mean for his future.

I was thinking about the future, and I asked to be sent a sign that all would be well. Just then one of those tiny willy wagtails hopped across the courtyard, ignored the other blokes sitting with me and stopped directly in front of me. Then it opened its wings right up and squawked directly at me. I've never seen anything like it before, and I hope it is a sign that everything one day will work out right.

The End of the Road

As this book is being written, Walsh is still in prison and Gemma is still essentially in prison with him. Twenty-five years of non-parole is up soon.

Walsh could move to another prison and enter another pre-release program, but he refuses to be separated from Gemma. She simply couldn't afford the weekly or even fortnightly petrol for the long trip to a new prison, and with the state of her health and the painkillers she's constantly taking, she's not sure she could drive that far anyway. In the meantime, they speak on the phone numerous times a day – here, prisoners are allowed to call out for 20 minutes at a time, as often as they wish, just so long as there is an hour between calls. From experience, Walsh knows that he'd be risking his life should he attempt to ring Gemma before 10 am. She is definitely not a morning person.

> But would you believe it? After all the campaigning we did elsewhere to get the phone calls extended, here they campaigned to get it cut shorter! They used to get longer, but some prisoners whose families didn't live locally complained that it was too long or too expensive or something so it got cut back.

And the prison here isn't so bad after the horrors of Walsh's original one. 'The boys will tell you that this prison is an old folks' holiday home. Sure, some prison officers are worse than others and there are always annoying things, but in general it is not too bad.'

Walsh agrees, but says that little annoyances or rules can still rankle when you're inside.

It's little things like them cancelling the annual Christmas barbecue. It used to be the one day of the year that I could sit and eat a meal with my wife, just like a normal couple, but then the prison just cancelled it. The prisoners used to save up all year for it too, so it is not like it was costing the system anything.

Walsh is also frustrated that he has not been allowed to continue the artwork that kept him sane for so many years elsewhere.

I'm not allowed to have the tools I need for that work. Even drawing or painting is difficult – I campaigned to be allowed to have the materials I needed, and they agreed but said that they had to be kept in a separate building. So every time I needed something new I had to leave the place where I was drawing and ask permission to get a new paintbrush or something. That kind of stuff gets really irritating after a while.

Tension between prisoners can also be a source of ongoing disruption. One night Walsh awoke to find that someone had set fire to another prisoner's mattress. Luckily the guy wasn't in bed at the time. And luckily, Walsh is a very large, very strong man. He was able to single-handedly fold the flaming mattress in half to smother the flames and carry it out onto the grass at the front, before raising the alarm.

Overall, Walsh considers that the accommodation isn't too bad. Most of the men are housed in cottages in the grounds of the prison. He has his own room – a luxury that he waited for.

When I first got to this prison, I said I didn't want to go out into the general population until I was sure of myself. But in reality, I just wanted to wait until there was a single room available!

If I'd gone straight out, I would have had to double up with someone.

In the cottage, they're allowed to cook for themselves too, and at the moment he's lucky enough to share his home with a guy who does a mean chicken casserole. On the phone each day, it's sharing with Gemma those kinds of details of everyday life that keeps him sane – and sharing the ongoing intricacies and the ever-present mountain of paperwork relating to his case.

'Gemma has been more supportive than you can believe', says Walsh. He relies on Gemma as someone who is there to listen when prison is getting him down, and when he is off-loading perhaps a little *too* much, she'll say the key phrase 'prison stuff'. That's his clue that he needs to lighten up.

The one interest they don't share is bingo. Gemma is a regular at games in the small town where she lives, but whenever games are organised for the prisoners inside, Walsh won't have a bar of them. 'I've been around here for a long time, and I've seen the trouble that games can cause. Gambling is a huge problem inside', he says. 'They'll bet on anything from a game of darts to bingo, and there is always trouble. It's best just to stay away from anything like that.'

Walsh and Gemma also differ on the idea of sitting down and watching a crime show for fun. 'I love them, but he won't watch them – particularly not anything with rape or murder in it. Sometimes I forget and I'll ask him whether he saw something on TV the night before, and he'll say, "You know I don't watch that shit".' But Greg does like films like *The Shawshank Redemption*; it makes him realise that his lot is not as bad as some.

Despite the setbacks they have experienced, Gemma and Walsh have plans and dreams for his eventual release. His plans for that very first day of freedom involve sitting on a blanket on Gemma's front lawn under the sky and talking about their future. He's looking forward to walking her kelpies – Charlie and Ella – and possibly a move to another state, a job and a new home with an open fire. Normal stuff. He's also planning on getting a licence – about 40 years after his first attempt. 'I failed my test when I sat it as a young guy, and I never bothered getting one despite owning lots of different cars', he admits. 'But when I get out, I'm going to do everything by the book. There's no way I want to end up back inside.'

Walsh clearly feels a little awkward discussing his dreams for his life outside. 'At the back of my mind there is always the thought of Louisa and the life she could have led.' But when pushed, he says that he'd like the freedom to sit in the sun and eat meals with his wife. He wants to learn reiki so he can help Gemma with the constant pain that has dogged her since her accident at work. And Gemma doesn't know this, so reading this chapter will doubtless come as a surprise, but he's also planning a few singing lessons.

> Before my arrest, I'd been at a bar one night and done some singing. I realised that I don't have a bad voice – well, I wasn't booed off stage – and I'd really enjoyed it. I still remember being in lockup a week later and looking out. That same bar I'd been singing at was directly across the road. What I'd like to do is learn to sing properly so I can sing for Gemma. It would be my way of showing her what she means to me.

Whatever the future may hold for them, singing lessons or more prison bars, Greg and Gemma Walsh are determined to stand by the vows they made to each other on the day of the wedding.

All that I am I give to you, and all that I have I share with you.

Whatever the future holds, I will love you and stand by you as long as we both shall live.

This is my solemn vow.

Chapter 7
Mind Games

The human desire to connect to others is a powerful force, and while strict regulations across the states and territories of Australia control interactions between prison staff and prisoners, not to mention prisoners and prisoners, it's not surprising that sometimes 'things' happen. Just like in the outside world, all sorts of factors can drive these relationships: power, boredom, better access to goodies, someone to listen, even genuine romantic attachment.

Sometimes, of course, it's about sexual gratification – even supposedly straight men and women will opt for sex however they can get it while inside, and then revert to heterosexuality on release ('gate gays' as they are sometimes described).

But relationships behind bars are not restricted to homosexual encounters, no matter what the prison authorities would like to believe. The days of only allowing staff of the same sex to guard prisoners have long gone, and not even headline events such as the romance between prisoner warden Heather Parker and inmate Peter Gibb are likely to change this. And then there are all the other people with access to inmates – the medical personnel, psychologists and rehabilitation-program coordinators. If you're inside, you're just as likely to see a young female domestic-violence course leader, as a male dentist or a female psychologist.

The Constant Craving

Access to members of the opposite sex was not something Frank had thought much about when he first went to prison, aged 18, for drug-related offences. He was firmly in the grip of heroin by then, and as the Australian Drug Foundation describes it:

> There is evidence that after prolonged use heroin is highly addictive. People who use heroin regularly can develop dependence and tolerance to it, which means they need to take larger amounts of heroin to get the same effect. Dependence on heroin can be psychological, physical, or both. People who are dependent on heroin find that using the drug becomes far more important than other activities in their life. They crave the drug and find it very difficult to stop using it.

For nearly 16 years, his relationship with heroin was going to be Frank's primary focus. Girls simply could not compete long-term with the drug he craved. He was young, hooked on heroin, and aside from the odd fling when outside, his experience of relationships was fairly limited.

> It wasn't too bad going to prison that first time, aside from the side-effects of not being able to use. Was I scared? Well, yes and no. Like many others, I got a protector when I first went in – a friend of my dad's who grabbed hold of me and looked after me.

He admits that his addiction and criminal history have been incredibly hard on his parents.

> They were probably at their most relieved – if not their happiest – whenever I was in jail. At least then, they knew where I was.

When I was out, I could be anywhere, or I could be dead. They knew when I was in jail, they'd at least get a phone call if there was a problem. They were at peace when I was in there.

Other friends of Frank in other jails found other protectors, such as the well-known underworld figure Nicolai Radev – also known as 'The Russian'. Radev had been jailed for assault, blackmail, threats to kill, extortion, firearm offences, armed robbery and drug charges, and was known to police as an enforcer for the Melbourne head of the Russian mafia and for robbing drug dealers. (Radev was later shot and killed in Queen Street, Coburg on 15 April 2003, one in a series of similar events known as the Melbourne gangland killings. He was shot seven times in the head and chest in front of his bodyguard after he got out of his black Mercedes Benz CLK 500 convertible – an expensive car he'd somehow been able to buy after just eight months of official income as a helper in a fish and chip shop during the 1980s.) Frank was lucky to have a family friend on hand instead.

That first time around, Frank had received a two-year term, with a one-year minimum (also known as a bottom). Little did he know that he was going to essentially spend the next decade or so of his life behind bars. By the end of it, Frank was an old hand himself. 'Now that mate of my dad's sort of looks up to me.'

There were lots of eye-opening experiences for Frank that first time, but as the years rolled past and he was out for a few weeks, back in for a few years, the prison routine became familiar. One of the fixed 'appointments' in his calendar was the regular visit to his psychologist.

Crossing The Line

More than a decade older than Frank, Jennifer was a trained psychologist employed by the prison. She was married with children.

But she was also to prove deeply disturbed herself, not only violating her professional relationship with a client, but also the trust of her employer, and many of the 31 pages of ethical guidelines outlined in the Australian Psychological Society's Code of Ethics.

'I'm not exactly sure when it started', Frank says. 'If I look back now, I reckon she was putting the moves on me for months before I finally realised what was happening. I hadn't had much experience of relationships then.'

Frank was booked in for a series of one-on-one sessions with the psychologist to discuss his personal issues, his rehabilitation and his plans for the future. Obviously, he divulged a lot of personal information during those sessions, but for most of the time, Jennifer maintained a professional silence about her own feelings or experiences. It was only as the end of their scheduled sessions was nearing that she began talking about her own life. One can only speculate about what was happening to drive the older psychologist to cross the boundary with the 22-year-old prisoner.

Frank is not so surprised that it happened, but wonders why she specifically targeted him.

Despite what people think, relationships do happen a lot between officers and prisoners. One of my friends has been in a relationship with a female officer for many years and still is to this day. He's been in for a long time and Rebecca hasn't changed jobs in that time – maybe so they can still see each other.

Frank's friend, Ric, is constantly playing up and being sent to segregation, where he is separated from other prisoners in a punishment cell or 'slot' as it is more commonly known in Australian prison slang. 'When he's down there, they get a chance to see each other more privately because there are not so many people running around in the unit. Everyone is locked in.'

Ric can be sent to the slot for a couple of months at a time, but for him the pain of punishment is obviously worth being able to see the woman he loves more regularly and more privately. As Frank describes it: 'It's natural to want to have that kind of connection to someone, and he has been in jail for a long, long time'.

Ric still has a couple of years of his sentence to serve, but when he is finally released, Frank is convinced that Ric and Rebecca will indeed end up together on the outside. 'To be honest, I'd have to say that they do genuinely love each other. Their relationship has been of no benefit to him – it's not like she has been doing him any major favours or anything; it was just for his own gratification, and the pleasure of spending time with her.'

Ric's partner isn't a low-ranking officer either. 'She's actually pretty high up, but because she cares for Ric, I don't think she cares if she is breaking the rules.' However, Frank does think that she would mind if she lost her job, which is probably the reason why the couple don't fraternise in front of others, and that only a very few close friends know about their relationship.

Behind Closed Doors

Frank says that he was initially shocked when his regular closed-door time with his psychologist began turning into something more like a flirtation than a therapeutic session. When she first came clean about how she fancied her handsome 22-year-old client, Frank says he panicked.

> I was tripping out because I knew that I could get in trouble for breaking the prison rules. She was from the outside and God knows what she could have brought in and given to me during our sessions. It's not like she *did* give me anything, but if there was any suspicion that she had, I would have ended up back in maximum security. She was a link to the outside that

they couldn't monitor in the same way as they did the guards. Anything could have happened. And if we'd been caught she would have lost her job too, of course.

Some of the things she said to Frank made him feel distinctly squeamish. 'She was pretty out there with what she talked about. She'd try to kiss me and all sorts of other stuff. And remember, we were in a room alone together for an hour at a time.'

It was wrong on all sorts of levels. Frank was in his twenties, she was much older; he was single, she was married with children. But most importantly, she was his therapist. She was being paid to look after Frank's psychological well-being, not to seduce him.

Jennifer's advances completely confused Frank. On the one hand, she really knew him, she had been listening to his darkest secrets for months. Plus she was female and interested in him. Opportunities like that don't come along all that often in prison. He wasn't in love exactly, but her passion was hard to resist.

Frank always knew that should their extra activities in the private room become public, she'd be in serious trouble both professionally and personally, particularly should her husband ever hear what she'd been up to at work. But Frank had other doubts about the relationship too.

After a while, it started doing my head in because I was still young and hadn't had many relationships. And I was starting to get annoyed because it was like she was playing games with me. It was only in the last few weeks that she spoke about her kids and husband and house and all the rest of it. But where was I going to fit into all that – in a sleepout out the back of their home? It was all too weird that she wanted an ongoing relationship with me. And the next thing I knew, she had resigned.

When Frank went in for his last session with Jennifer, she wouldn't go near him. He thinks now that she was worried about the prison authorities and that someone might walk in and find them in a compromising position. Frank is fairly convinced that this was paranoia – if the room had been bugged, which would be a violation of his role as a patient, he thinks – then someone would have interrupted them long before this final session. And it was kind of annoying for him too. If she was really leaving, why would she care if he approached her in the room during their last session? Why would she care if they were caught red-handed? Her behaviour was a complete head spinner for a naive 22-year-old.

From Therapist to Stalker

Not even Jennifer's new job outside the prison and her lack of an excuse to see Frank professionally could dampen her passion. She began writing long, weekly letters, some of which he still has today. Frank says that he was still intrigued by what was going on. 'OK, I was a bit naive, but I was young and the weirdness of it all didn't really strike me till later.'

The letters included pages and pages about how she was going to leave her husband and kids, how she would pick him up when he was released, and then they'd be together. 'She was clearly after a full-on relationship', says Frank. 'She also kept sending me money – $150 a month – and books too.'

Oddly enough, the books were all about fatherhood, and how to be a good dad. One cover he remembers featured a man holding a baby. Frank is still rather bemused by the relevance. He didn't have kids then, and he still doesn't now. He can only think that perhaps she was hoping to have kids with him, despite her age.

I felt like she was looking at me as a potential sperm donor or something. That she'd been looking through all the prisoners and looked for the best donor. The whole thing was totally weird, and her letters were even stranger. I couldn't get my head around the idea that we'd seen each other for an hour at a time each week and suddenly she was just going to leave everything in her life for me. That she was prepared to leave her husband and kids for someone she'd known for such a little time. I can only think she wanted me to be her toy boy or something.

Jennifer never visited Frank after she resigned from her job at the prison. And after she'd left, he started hearing odd stories about her from other prisoners. He didn't hear of anyone who'd had a similar experience to his, but he heard that she had given other prisoners contraband items, such as chocolate biscuits. 'She could have lost her job over that alone. And when I heard about the chockie biscuits, I couldn't help thinking that I'd rather those than a book on fatherhood!'

Frank didn't respond to many of her letters; the few that he did send were posted to her at her place of work rather than to her home.

In the end, I was sick of it. I'd had enough, thanks. In my last letter to her, I told her that it wasn't going to work, and she had to understand the reason why I hadn't been writing back or seeming interested. She had seen something in me that she wanted, but that it wasn't reciprocated. I'd been intrigued with her persistence and interest in me, but that was it. In the end, it came down to the fact the whole relationship had been one-sided.

Double Detox

Today, Frank has been clean of heroin and out of jail for three years, an achievement for which his new girlfriend, Amber, jokingly claims credit. There's probably more than a word of truth in it. As Frank describes it, she is his crutch and is very good to him, 'even when I am a pain in the arse'.

It probably helps that Amber knew exactly what he was going through when he finally escaped the drug scene to get clean; she did it alongside him.

'I actually met my girl through the drug scene, but we then moved away from it together. We are very lucky', says Frank. And Amber is very lucky that Frank's experience with his psychologist in prison hasn't damaged his long-term ability to love and trust another female.

'He told me from the start that he never wanted a girlfriend. "We can never be", he said. I thought it was because he knew my son's father, but no, it was because he didn't want any kind of relationship', says Amber. But since the day they first got together, the two have never been apart – not even for a night.

Frank says, 'We get along brilliantly and I couldn't ever see myself being with anyone else. I probably annoy the shit out of her I know, but we both were heroin addicts for a long time, so we understand each other like no-one else can.'

Both were ready to leave the drug scene behind. 'Frank just turned up at our place one day and told me to get ready – we were going to move in with his parents and get clean.' The two left everything behind . . . their home, their possessions, and their friends. They finished off the last of the gear (heroin) they had at hand, and spent the next few days lying next to each other in Frank's old bedroom at home, fighting off the worst of the withdrawal symptoms. And detoxing from heroin is not a pleasant experience. Again, according to the Australian Drug Foundation:

If a dependent person stops taking heroin, or severely cuts down the amount they use, they will experience withdrawal symptoms because their body has to get used to functioning without heroin.

Symptoms can start within 6 to 24 hours after the last dose. Heroin withdrawal symptoms usually peak within 1 to 3 days and gradually subside in 5 to 7 days. Some of the withdrawal symptoms that may be experienced include: cravings for heroin, restlessness, yawning, increased irritability, depression, crying, diarrhoea, low blood pressure . . .

And all that's before you get to the stomach and leg cramps, the muscle spasms, the vomiting, goose bumps, runny nose, insomnia, loss of appetite and elevated heart rate.

I didn't think we could do it, to be honest. Well, I thought that she might be able to, but not me. And I really didn't think it would work both of us coming off it at the same time. I knew that if one of us caved in, the other one would too. Luckily, the symptoms only last a couple of weeks these days because the quality of the gear is crap, not like years ago when it was very strong.

Amber has nothing but praise for Frank's strength during their detox. 'We were both really sick, and Frank was very fidgety. But he did so well. I thought he'd go completely crazy, because he had always been such a pig for heroin, using thousands of dollars a day.'

Frank had always supported his habit by dealing in drugs – hence his lengthy stretches in prison – and he admits that of the $5000 he was making a day at one stage, practically all of it went straight into his arm. However, he had a few stints of being clean – usually forced into it when he was in the police lock up and had no access to the drugs he craved.

'When you've in the police cells for a couple of weeks, you've already hung out (detoxed) by the time you go to prison, so it's pointless then going onto methadone in there.' Unless, of course, you get back onto heroin, and Frank is swift to point out that at one stage he was using every day inside.

> You'd think there wouldn't be drugs in prison, but there's probably more in there than in the community. If they are not going to stop drugs getting into prisons, the least they could do is give prisoners needles and syringes to stop them sharing and protect them from AIDS and hepatitis.

Getting off the gear was a slow and painful process – nothing like the experience Amber had one time before when she flew to Israel with her then boyfriend and his father for a 'rapid detox'.

> We used before we got on the plane and by the time we got to Rome airport, my boyfriend and I were so sick that we were just lying on the floor of the airport, unable to move. His dad rang the doctor in Israel who told him just to get us on the plane and to see him as soon as we arrived.

Amber and her boyfriend were given morphine tablets for the pain. 'We took them by the handful!' Then the next day they were sedated and given a full blood transfusion to rid their bodies of all the heroin byproducts. 'When I woke up eight hours later, it was like I had never ever used. I was almost turning somersaults, I felt so good.' Once out of hospital, Amber took a side trip to Jerusalem from Tel Aviv. 'It is the most beautiful city – being there after the detox, I felt like the devil was coming out of me.'

Sadly, despite the $60,000 cost of the treatment and its initial success, Amber went back onto heroin six months later, after her boyfriend beat her up. 'I should have left him when I got off that plane.' She admits that when things go wrong in her life, heroin has always been her comfort. Now she and Frank have each other.

Frank also realises the importance of the support they give each other.

> After we first got off the gear, a couple of months went by, then a couple more, and suddenly we were clear. It has been three years now and it is the best thing I have ever done. We keep each other strong – on days when I'm not feeling good, she's there for me and I do the same for her. We're like a crutch for each other.

'People can't believe Frank is the same person when they see him today, now that he is off the gear', says Amber. The only mementos she has to show for her time on drugs are a lot of bad memories and two large white scars across her stomach and upper thigh, where a blocked femoral artery – caused by her years of heroin usage – was replaced with another functioning artery from her tummy.

Frank's scars are not physical, but are there nonetheless – the result of his years of imprisonment and his experiences inside. He admits that having spent over a decade of his life in prison – practically all of his adult life – he could probably be described as institutionalised.

Amber describes his difficulty leaving the house or facing new situations as social phobia. 'He doesn't like going out in the street or having strangers around. He thinks they are looking at him or talking about him, and will say things like, "What are YOU looking at?", even if what they were doing was completely unintended.'

Even a simple trip to the supermarket has its fears for Frank. 'When I send him to the supermarket for something, he never goes up and down the aisles browsing like a normal person. He just goes straight to what he needs and gets out quickly.'

Amber was also very worried by his habit, when he first got out of jail, of always carrying a knife or box-cutter or screwdriver around with him.

> It was a hangover from jail, where he always had to be alert in case he was attacked. When he first got out, he assumed it was the same here. I was always telling him to put the knife down, asking him why he felt he had to carry it. I was really worried because if he'd been stopped by the police, he would have been straight back inside for sure.

In most states in Australia, partners receive little information on what it will be like for their loved ones when they are released – not to mention how they might behave and warning signs to look out for. Those like Frank, who've spent significant time in jail, face considerable challenges adjusting to everyday life. Rarely are they given the chance to escape their past.

Amber sometimes gets tired of it too:

> It's not like being an ordinary citizen. If Frank is pulled over by the police for any reason, they don't just want his name; when they get that, then they want to go through absolutely everything, including his criminal history from 10 years ago. And he is not the same person now. He is labelled for life even now that his life is back on track.

The one element of his life that is not yet sorted is employment. When he first got out, Frank worked with his father and brother in the family business for nearly two years, but the dynamics proved difficult so he needed to leave. But it is difficult to find a job when you have a record, says Frank.

All employers want to know what your background is and whether you have ever been in trouble. What can I say about where I was for 10 years of my adult life? I don't have a proper work history, as I'd only be out of prison for a couple of weeks or perhaps a month. I'd get caught dealing again and then I'd be back inside for a few more months or years.

Amber has started a certificate course in welfare, and is hopeful that maybe Frank will do something similar – perhaps in the field of drug and alcohol counselling. After all, it is something he knows about from the inside out.

I reckon Frank would be a great counsellor. He'd be able to empathise with the clients and they are hardly going to look at him and say that he has no idea what he is talking about. He'll also know when they are trying to bullshit him. It wouldn't be like he had just read a book on the side effects of getting off heroin and was pretending he knew it all.

Experience is something that Frank does feel passionate about.

Parole officers and anyone working with prisoners or ex-prisoners need to have life experience. The 22-year-olds don't have a clue. When they first start, they are all happy-go-lucky, rosy-cheeked and gullible. They have no idea what is going on. After a while, they learn what is what and they realise that most of the people who have been nice to them have only done it to get around them in some way. When they finally learn that, they feel as if they have been played and turn into arseholes. The best are those that have been around for a while and can immediately spot who is going to be trouble. The older ones are much more easygoing because they understand that it is just a big game that everyone plays – it is us against them.

Frank is equally passionate about prison reform and drug rehabilitation. He's been there, done that, and quite frankly, his time in prison just taught him more about the drug trade. Getting off drugs and staying clean is something he did all by himself.

Jails don't work. They just house people and get them off the streets. Putting everyone in together means that the ones who aren't so bad, look to the others and become as bad, if not worse. From experience, I know that going to prison means you just acquire more knowledge about crime. And instead of helping people with the problem that got them into prison in the first place, they [the prison staff] do nothing.

Frank allows that most people in prison deserve to be there for what they have done, but he argues that many are really there because of their addiction, whether it be drugs, gambling or alcohol.

Instead of building four jails costing $600 million, why don't they just build three jails and spend the money they save on programs that really help people with their problems? It would help huge numbers of prisoners and save them a shitload of money because people like me wouldn't spend years in and out of prison.

He has a valid point. One can only hope that someone gives him a chance for employment now too.

Chapter 8
Blight

Once a keen amateur theatre player, David Peri was about to embark on his third stage performance for the Plan B Theatre Project, a theatre company set up to help former inmates reconnect with the outside world. First he'd had the title role in a play called *'Til Hell Freezes*, about a man doing a lengthy sentence in prison. Then he'd had another key role in *Rock 'n' a Hard Place*, described as a 'ghost ride through an emotional landscape of captivity'. That play had been staged in the old City Watch House on Russell Street in Melbourne, which, until 1996, was a halfway house on the slippery slope into Victoria's prison system. During the course of that play, the action moved through the various eerie parts of the watch house, from the entrance to the assembly areas to the cells, tracking a group of prisoners, including first-timers and old hands.

But the setting for his third appearance, in a play called *Blight*, was quite surreal for Peri. The dock of Courtroom 12 of the old Supreme Court, where he now stood in front of an audience, was exactly where he had stood 20 years earlier facing a charge of murder.

This time around, he was wearing a long black cape and a full mask, rather like the Phantom of the Opera. The first time, he was dressed rather more soberly, but it didn't stop the judge from sending him down.

Me and a friend of mine had gone out and shot a bloke with, let's just say, a rather large weapon. We got done a couple of days later because we left the body lying in the bush rather than burying it and a guy who was out hunting with some mates found the body by fluke.

When we shot the guy, he fell over and somehow one knee was left sticking up – maybe caught on a log or something. The hunter happened to be looking at the same patch of bush through a scope and he saw a flash of blue from our guy's jeans. He didn't realise it was a body, but the blue colour stuck in his mind, unfortunately. When he came back down after a day's shooting, he went to have a look at what that blue thing had been and bingo – he found the body. Very unfortunately for us, as it turned out.

Centre Stage

Peri was always going to be high on the police's list of suspects, as the victim was shortly due to testify against him in another case. But to seal his fate, a friend of Peri's – ex-friend nowadays, unsurprisingly – rang the police and dobbed him in. Peri doesn't know where his ex-friend may be now – as far as Peri is aware, he is tucked safely out of the way in witness protection.

On his last day of freedom, Peri's wife, Eve, was at work and his five-year-old son, Joe, was at school. Peri was home alone when he took a phone call from his solicitor telling him that the police were on their way and that he should make himself scarce.

To this day, I think that call from the solicitor was a set up. Of course, I went straight around to my mate's place and, of course, the cops followed me. They then surrounded the caravan park where he was living. His girlfriend had gone out for a moment – to do the laundry or something – and when the door to the caravan opened, we didn't think anything of it, just assumed it was her returning. But then we looked up and there was a big guy standing there with a gun. It was a cop. Looking back on it, we deserved to get caught.

The first that Eve knew about her husband's arrest was when the police rang her at work. Peri insists that she had known nothing about the murder, or even that he was a career thief: 'Gawd, I wouldn't have told her anything like that! Let's just say that she didn't react well!'

It certainly didn't help matters that the day of Peri's arrest was the couple's wedding anniversary. Even though they hadn't planned anything special for the night, having your husband arrested for murder can't rate highly on the scale of anniversary celebrations. 'The second of June will always carry a double whammy for me', says Peri. 'One of the best days of my life and one of the worst.'

Eve was very upset, as you'd expect. I told her that I was innocent, of course, and of course she believed me. I'd always hoped that somehow I would get bail and then get found 'not guilty' – neither of which ended up happening. She was totally shattered when I got convicted and sent down.

Peri did eventually tell Eve that he *had* been responsible for the murder, but as shocked as she was, she vowed to stand by him. They loved each other, after all.

At that stage Peri and Eve had been married for six years, they had a small child together, another on the way, and all the trappings of a happily married life. Much of it had been acquired by thieving. 'I was a very, very, very good thief', says Peri. 'I never got caught for thieving – anything I wanted became mine.' As part of his career, he also developed a very good understanding of the law. 'I studied it – mainly so I could break it more efficiently.'

These days, Peri also knows quite a bit more about the prison system than he would like. His original sentence was for life but, as he explains it, life doesn't necessarily mean life. 'It depends on the number they put on the bottom [the non-parole period].'

In New South Wales, they're tough. They'll say life with 90 years on the bottom, which means that the poor bastard *will* be in for life unless he was like three years old when he went in. But in Victoria back in the 1980s, it was much more lenient. One guy in Pentridge with me stabbed a guy 117 times – now that was overkill in my book. It was all over getting his pay packet, and he only did 12 years.

You have to do something really evil to get a real life sentence. Like that girl who was recently murdered in Werribee – the guy who's accused of killing her had done it before to someone else. Being of a criminal mindset myself, I reckon he's a sicko and will probably end up with a sentence like Carl Williams. Not that Carl Williams will be serving out his sentence any more, of course!'

(While serving a life sentence with a 35-year non-parole period for four murders, notorious underworld identity Carl Williams, 39, was beaten to death with the stem of an exercise bike by another inmate, Matthew Charles Johnson, in Barwon Prison's maximum-security Acacia unit.)

The Supporting Role

A quietly spoken man with a dry sense of humour, Peri doesn't discount how difficult it must have been for his wife to know that she was effectively going to be a single mother. 'We loved each other and had a really strong connection, so it was very hard knowing that we were going to be separated for the next 18 years.'

Eve also had to deal with their family and friends, many of whom had found out about Peri's fate through the headlines in the papers. 'A few were fine; others not so. Some people said that they would have expected me to do an armed robbery or something, but not to do a murder. I don't know whether that is good or bad. Either way, they weren't surprised that I was into criminal things.'

The loneliness and sense of loss was the hardest part of those early days in prison, Peri says. 'Not only did I have to put up with the crap that was going on in prison, I also had to worry about Eve and how she was coping without me.' His main concern at the time was the safety of his pregnant wife and son.

> People had put notes in her letterbox saying 'an eye for an eye, a son for a son', and I was powerless to protect Eve and my son from inside. In the end, nothing ended up happening – we were dealing with cowards after all – but it was a pretty low act to threaten the life of a woman and child. She ended up moving house.

Peri missed the birth of his second child.

> I remember the moment when the screws came to the door of the dormitory I was in and congratulated me, saying that my wife had delivered a baby daughter. Of course, I would rather have been there with my wife for the birth, but circumstances didn't allow.

Giving birth aside, Peri admits that it is never easy for the one on the outside – there is lots of running around to do, and financially it can be very difficult too, particularly if a woman needs to support her partner in prison.

Work in Victorian prisons is an option, not a rule, and Peri says that many prisoners don't bother, instead relying upon their wife or girlfriend or family to put money in their account every month so they have money to spend. 'I was different. I worked all through the sentence so I had money.' Peri is a tailor by trade – a very good tailor, he points out with a refreshing lack of modesty. In each of the prisons where he lived he gravitated naturally to the sewing division, ending up as head tailor on a number of occasions. As well as his prison salary, he'd make extra on the side by sewing clothes for other prisoners.

> People would want nice clothes for their visits. The tracksuits they used to have back then didn't have side pockets, so I used to customise them with side pockets and pleats down the middle. Or I'd turn round-necked jumpers into V-necks. We also made proper fitted overcoats for winter . . . double-breasted, lovely numbers.

In return, Peri would be paid in cigarettes (back when he still smoked) or in tins of coffee. 'The screws used to wonder why I had such a large collection of coffee tins, and I used to pretend that I'd forgotten I had any, so had gone and bought yet some more.'

He could take care of himself financially, but he needed Eve to provide other, much-needed support. Visits – while eagerly anticipated – were heart wrenching.

> We were always surrounded by other people, so we couldn't express what we really wanted to express, or do what we really wanted to do. We could hold hands, but that was about it. There are limits to what else you can legally do in a prison waiting room . . . although some people did push the boundaries!

For most of the 15 years I was inside, she visited me, but it was difficult when I was moved to Loddon because she didn't drive. We were always on the phone though.

Trust wasn't an issue. 'We were married, for heaven's sake! And I wasn't like some of the other blokes that I'd hear on the phone to their girlfriends', says Peri.

You get some guys who are real standovers. They'll be on the phone demanding things and ordering her to do this and that, and threatening that if she didn't then she'd get bashed when he got out.

I always used to hear conversations like that and think: 'You don't deserve to have a girlfriend, you fucking idiot. You don't talk to someone like that, when they are sticking by you. I could never work out why women stood by men like that.

From Small Beginnings

Peri blames the Christian Brothers for his descent into a life of crime —not that he was sexually abused as others were. Indeed, his first brush with the label 'thief' came when, aged seven, he and some mates were rummaging around in the hard-rubbish collection to see if any of the neighbours had discarded anything interesting. Inside one screw-top tin, Peri found a massive set of old-fashioned keys.

I thought they were pretty special so I took the keys home and showed my parents. Then I took it to primary school to show my mates, and one of the teachers, Miss Ross, took them away from me. Her name is still burned into my memory and I don't care if she reads this. She was an old hag back then and probably dead now.

Peri was called up to the principal's office.

> His name was Brother Dillon, a tall skinny bloke with Superman glasses. He asked me where I got the keys and I told him. He asked again and I told him again. He was getting angrier and angrier. Eventually, he yelled: 'Do you know what these keys are for, you little thief? They open all the doors of the school.'

Peri was given the strap and went home feeling awful. 'Believe it or not, I was a good kid back then and I was completely humiliated by being called a thief by the brother.'

He confessed all to his parents, who spent the weekend questioning neighbours about the keys.

> It turned out the tin with the keys inside had been accidentally thrown out by an old woman whose husband used to be the caretaker years before at the school. On the Monday morning, my dad went to school and tore strips off Brother Dillon for calling me a liar. I got a half-arsed apology but it was then that my mind started to twist.

The real turning point for Peri came one day in another class with Brother Donahue, when a classmate's fountain pen stopped working.

> Brother Donahue was a bad-tempered prick and he told Ricky Holloway to shut up, throw the pen in the bin and sit down. During recess, I stayed back, took the pen out of the waste-paper basket, found the blockage and cleared it. I then tested it to see if it now worked and when it did, I put it in my desk. I thought nothing more about it. The pen had been chucked away and I had fixed it.

Before school finished, the brother had calmed down and told Ricky he could get his pen out of the bin.

> Of course it wasn't there, so he asked who had taken it and honest me puts my hand up. 'Oh', he says. 'We have a thief in the class.' He got a piece of A4 cardboard and with a thick black pen wrote, 'I am a thief', on it, then hung it round my neck with some string and paraded me through every classroom of the school. That was the start of it all. I thought if they are going to accuse me of being a thief, I might as well be the best one I can possibly be.

Looking back now, Peri admits these might seem like small incidents, but he says that to a good little Catholic kid, they were devastating.

Exit Eve Stage Left

There are a lot of wannabe toughs inside, Peri says.

> Muscles are a big thing especially with the younger ones. They spend all day and night at the gym and by the time they get out, they look like they have balloons hanging off them. It's funny because some of them come in as skinny as a beanpole from drugs; inside, they pump themselves up and become big gangsters, but when they get out they get into the gear again and become skinny little beanpoles again.

You get used to seeing the same old faces time and time again, explains Peri. 'There were guys in there who didn't care whether they were in or out – they'd be released and shortly after you'd see them back again. "Plan A didn't work out", they'd say.' There was also one old homeless guy who used to do anything to get into prison over the Christmas period. 'He just wanted somewhere nice to sleep and something to eat.'

Inside prison is a whole different ball game. 'It's a world of its own, with the haves and have-nots, the wannabes and the ones who really are. The wannabes are the ones you see strutting about.' And if there is a pecking order, the paedophiles are right down the bottom, kept away from the mainstream population in protection. 'And then you have those in protection from the protection prisoners!'

Peri's early experience in amateur theatre doubtless stood him in good stead. In an interview with *The Age* in 2005, at the time of his role in *Rock 'n' a Hard Place*, he described how prison life helped make him an actor, as he'd learned to behave one way with his fellow prisoners, another way with prison guards, and as 'a diplomat' with the Parole Board.

For Peri, the toughest part of being inside was the lack of privacy. 'I hated sharing a cell with anyone else. I got used to it, but I never liked it. If you're in with an idiot who thinks he owns the whole cell and you're not allowed to do anything without his permission, then there's likely to be trouble and often is.' Peri is still bemused by the fact that some guys actually like doubling up.

> One guy I knew left a single cell to move in with someone else, simply because he liked having the company. You can't usually pick who you are put with, but if you get to know someone and get on well, and their cell mate is going to move out, then you can apply to move in.

Peri knows it would surprise most people to hear about what goes on behind some of those closed doors.

> In one place there was a jail cat who used to do all kinds of things for people. They had a whole system worked out where the jail

cat and his bloke of the moment would go into a cell and then hand the keys out through the trap to a lookout so they could be locked in for privacy. When they'd finished whatever they'd been doing, they'd just knock on the trap and be let out. It took me by surprise some of the well-known guys I used to see going in there!

Peri's sentence for murder was nearing its end, and Eve had been with him all the way. She'd also been the one in charge of child-rearing. 'As I wasn't there, she brought the kids up pretty much as she wanted. In a way, it's probably a good thing I wasn't there to influence it or God knows how the kids would have turned out.'

During the long years of separation, the couple had often talked about what they would do when they were together again. A holiday was at the top of the list – just the two of them – and then perhaps a move to a new place where they could start afresh.

Three years before the end of his sentence, Peri had been allowed to start a job on the outside, and was also allowed occasional leave. 'I'd meet my wife in town, help her with the shopping, get to see the children.'

Peri began making enthusiastic plans for leave they could spend at home. And that's when Eve dropped her bombshell.

Over the phone, she told me that she didn't want me to come back home after all. I was completely taken by surprise and completely devastated. I'd thought that we were going all right – I had no reason to think otherwise – and then all of a sudden she ended it. She just said she didn't want me back. It was my lowest point ever. I still loved her – still do, in fact – but she didn't love me.

It was almost worse when Peri found out from his son that there was no-one else involved. 'He said that she was just by herself. So it wasn't someone else – it was just me.' (He now thinks that Eve had been thinking about ending the marriage for some time, but didn't want to hurt him. It was the prospect of Peri coming home on leave that drove her to come clean.)

> I think that she'd got her life together over the time I was inside and didn't want it disrupted by me. It would have been very difficult for her having me walk in and try and get my place back in the family. She'd been head of the family for nearly 20 years – half a lifetime.

As a result of losing his wife, Peri also lost his much-prized outside job. As a man without a 'stable family' he was now considered a security risk. 'I wouldn't have tried to escape, having already done 15 years and with only three to go, but it was just one of their rules. I told them that I wouldn't try to escape, but they didn't believe me – they're bureaucrats after all, and they don't even believe each other.' Peri spent the remaining three years of his sentence inside. By himself.

The Second Stretch

His marriage over and his jail sentence behind him, Peri kept in touch with a few friends that he'd met on the inside. 'I became involved with one guy who thought it would be a very good idea if we made money by growing some dope.'

Unsurprisingly, it wasn't a good idea at all.

> I rented a house and we went out and bought all the gear we needed. One night, my mate Steve was going to bring some of the gear back to my house. He said he'd do it after dark because

he didn't want some cop pulling up alongside and seeing all the drug paraphernalia in the back of the car. He said that if he . hadn't rung me by a certain time, just to go to bed.

Peri hadn't heard from Steve by bedtime, so he simply unlocked the gates at the end of the long driveway and retired for a snooze. 'Next thing I know I heard a banging noise on the large glass sliding door at the back of the house and Steve was yelling, "Dave, where are you?"'

Rather than going out through the sliding door, Peri decided to take a short cut through the laundry and into the carport, where he fully expected to see loads of tubs and lights and other drug gear waiting to be unloaded. 'Instead I was greeted by the sight of a body in the carport. The whole place was covered in blood – my car, the walls, everything.'

While Peri had been sleeping, Steve had killed a man whom he owed $15,000. Murder must have seemed like an easy way of cancelling the debt. Peri reluctantly helped clean up the mess, but after a few months he decided to confess to the police.

The main thing was the guilt of being involved in such a thing. It was driving me crazy so I decided to go to the police. I thought about writing them an anonymous letter saying where the body was, but decided that was no good – they'd never be able to find it. So I went out to where the body was buried and put a big rock and a stick to mark the grave. I knew that if I told them to look for that, they'd be able to spot it.

David Peri was charged with being an accessory after the fact, and allowed out on bail until the case was heard. But what really got his goat was that the Director of Public Prosecutions used the statement he had willingly given police to charge him with all sorts of other crimes as well. 'They had no evidence of the drug-growing operation or guns, because obviously I'd got rid of all the evidence by then, but I still went down for those despite my statement being the only proof they had.'

Peri did three years. And the murderer? In the end, the man who'd dispatched his debtor in Peri's carport got off scot-free. The jury didn't believe Peri's account of what had happened.

Even though Peri ratted Steve out to police, he's not scared of Steve taking revenge. 'If he's out to get me, he'd be walking a very dangerous path! Of course, he'd be pissed off, but he wouldn't be stupid enough to try anything, shall we say. You don't survive all those years in prison without learning to handle yourself.'

Not much scares Peri these days. 'You become desensitised to violence after a while. I've seen stuff on the internet that is unbelievable, and it doesn't worry me at all. But I don't like maggots and I don't like heights. If I'm after you, my only tip is to get up high somewhere.'

The one good thing that came out of that second arrest was that it turned a switch in Peri's head and he finally gave up smoking.

I was standing outside the police car with two detectives and asked if I could have a smoke. After I finished, they took me down to the cells under the court – the yellow submarine they call it. When I was down there going through reception, they offered to get me an emergency kit, with cigarettes, toothbrush, anything else I might need. I just said, 'No, I don't smoke'. And I stopped just like that. It's expensive being a smoker in jail in any case.

The three years Peri spent back in prison were not in the mainstream prison population, but in protection. This was for his own safety, because he had been a witness in a trial. 'Those three years were harder than the 18 years I did in mainstream. It completely demoralised and destroyed me, mainly because I was stuck in there all sorts of people I wouldn't ordinarily mix with – paedos, rapists, you name it.'

There may have been other violent offenders in there too, he admits, or perhaps someone who hadn't paid a debt in the mainstream prison, but you had no way of easily knowing what someone had done. 'You can find out; it's not that hard. But it is considered bad manners to ask someone what they are in for. Only if you really get on well with someone might you say something like, 'By the way, what brought you here?''

The Last Act

When Peri went back to prison the second time, he sent Eve a Christmas card wishing her well, but the only reply that came back was a simple note from the post office saying that she was no longer at that address. They haven't had any contact since, despite sharing two children and the many years Eve spent supporting Peri during his first prison sentence.

Peri's son Joe was also deeply annoyed when he ended up back in prison again – after all, he'd been an absentee father for most of Joe's childhood and teenage years, but the pair have since reconciled. Peri is particularly proud that his son made it as a world-champion kickboxer, but worries over Joe's health after he picked up a mysterious bug during in a competition in Asia. 'They've got no idea what it is, and it is debilitating for Joe being in constant pain.'

'My daughter Lucy grew up without ever really having a father figure, but she is a beautiful woman both in looks and personality. She is a teacher and is also involved in corporate law – their mother did a fantastic job of bringing them up.'

Now living in regional New South Wales, David Peri has a new fiancé, and says that should she ever end up in prison, not that he thinks there's any chance of that, he'd definitely stick by her. 'I'd visit her all the time, get whatever she needed, look after her post and all that. I wouldn't just say, "Fuck you", you're a prisoner, I'm off.' It's only in recent times that he has learned how to trust again – and only a very few people at that.

He is even hoping to get back into the tailoring business soon. Men's clothes only, he says, none of that frilly women's stuff. 'I'm not one for wedding dresses. Bugger that, it would drive me insane!' He'd also like to get back into acting again. Perhaps he could reprise his role as the Phantom in *Phantom of the Opera*, or even one of his personal favourites – the role of the Police Sergeant in *Pirates of Penzance*. The blokes who arrested him would probably enjoy that performance. Maybe Eve would too, Peri thinks. 'I still love her, even though she no longer loves me.'

Chapter 9
Going Straight

Growing up with two violent and alcoholic criminals for parents, Chris reckons he didn't have much of a chance of a normal life. He was just seven years old when his father gave him 163 lashes with the buckle end of his leather belt, tried unsuccessfully to drown him, then dragged him up to the local police station and told the duty sergeant that Chris was no longer wanted by his parents. 'Dad went to prison for a month for the beating he'd given me. And I was sent to a children's home.'

At the home, Chris came to the attention of one of the male staff members, who showed him lots of attention – something that Chris craved. That attention soon turned to sexual abuse, but at the time, Chris felt that any attention was better than none. Besides, who would he tell? Another staff member? His parents? There was no-one he could trust.

Interstate, another small boy was growing up in equally horrific circumstances. 'My mother remarried and my stepfather made me eat meals out of a dog bowl in the corner of the kitchen', says Brad. As he grew up, Brad too was in and out of correctional facilities, and whenever he could, he took to the streets. Anything was better than life at home, or so he'd always imagined.

Chris believes that Brad's experiences in childhood and as a street kid would haunt anyone for the rest of their life. 'Is it any wonder he takes drugs when he has that sort of background? I say to people all the time, "Don't judge him until you really know him, because if you knew what he has been through, you'd have to think that he has done pretty well".'

Brad even says that he doesn't have any malice towards his stepfather, and that the man obviously had problems of his own. 'Yes, I'd shake his hand if I met him on the street.' Chris doesn't think that he could be so forgiving himself.

For a while, the young Chris's life took a turn for the better when he was fostered out of the children's home (ironically, given his later career path, by two married police officers). Jim was involved in search and rescue, and his wife Jenny was involved in community policing. Chris appreciates them, even if things didn't work out. 'They were lovely people, and they taught me right from wrong for the first time in my life, but coming from my background, I was always going to be trouble.' Things may have turned out differently had Jim and Jenny been able to adopt Chris, as they wished, and give him a permanent home, but Chris's mother said no. Chris was her son. Even if her husband had beaten him sufficiently to merit a jail sentence, she wasn't going to give him away to someone else. For the next few years, Chris ricocheted between foster care and the children's home.

At 14, after leaving the children's home for the final time, Chris was taken in by his paternal grandmother.

I was basically cast out by my parents, but my grandmother was a saint. She was a housekeeper for the Catholic priests from the 1950s until 1985, and always stood by me, even when I was in trouble. When my mum told her that I was gay, hoping to get a reaction, my grandmother turned around and said it didn't matter – that even if I had killed someone, she'd stand by me.

Chris's grandmother cared for him throughout his turbulent teens, then as old age and ill health took their toll, he cared for her until her death when he was 34.

Chris had been in trouble throughout his adolescence, mainly for petty shoplifting and vandalism. He'd also ended up losing touch with Jim and Jenny – his fault, not theirs, he is careful to say.

> I was embarrassed about the life I was leading and didn't want to bring shame on them. But whatever I may have done after that, I don't think I've done too badly, coming from a childhood like mine. I have made the best of what I have been given to work with.

One day Chris would like to write a book about his life. The working title is *Life with no Destiny*, and he plans to tell all the details of what he has been through over the years. He's not going to name names, but he says that people will be able to work out who they are. 'Their consciences will make them remember what they have done to me.'

What's In a Name?

Chris's sister, Tania, was killed on her 12th birthday, Anzac Day 1986, by a family friend who had known her all her short life. The family friend had been having sex with her, had made her pregnant, and now wanted to cover his tracks.

In newspaper reports from the time, the defense said that the killer, who pleaded not guilty, was a 'borderline defective with a mental age below that of a 10 year old'. The court was told that Tania was wearing the tracksuit he'd given her as a birthday present when she was blown off his bed by the force of a shot to the face.

In court, the killer said that the shooting had been an accident and that he loved Tania like a daughter. But the judge said that he believed Tania had been killed because she might reveal who had made her pregnant. (In fact, she was no longer pregnant, having had a miscarriage shortly before her death.)

Chris's mother had also been bashed to within an inch of death by the same neighbour. He'd asked her over to his home, shortly after murdering Tania, and had beaten her with the same weapon he'd used to kill Tania. 'My mother still suffers from her injuries today', says Chris. 'She's only four foot eleven and a half, and fought him with everything she had to stay alive.'

The killer was given 20 years, with a minimum of 14 years. 'He stood up in the court, and told the judge that he had every intention of killing the rest of the family too, and that they couldn't keep him locked up forever', says Chris. However, Tania's murderer was kept inside for the full length of his term, and was released 20 years later, in 2007. 'And this is a guy who blatantly put a double-barreled shotgun to a 12-year-old girl's face and pulled the trigger.'

During one of the killer's pre-release day outings, Tania's mother, Ivy, came face to face with her daughter's killer at a local shopping centre. For someone who'd been nearly killed herself by the same man, it was a chilling and incredibly distressing encounter, particularly given the threats he'd made in court and the pain she experienced every day since her attack.

Chris also encountered his sister's killer – behind bars.

One prison officer had never liked me, so when my sister's murderer changed divisions in Pentridge, the officer walked him right past me in front of the fence. I was still hurting badly for her, so it was a particularly horrible thing to do. I was still suffering post-traumatic shock at the time, and didn't know how to react. I didn't know whether I wanted to kill the man who'd done that to my sister or ask him why he had done it.

Chris still lives with the aftermath of Tania's murder. 'Since Tania was killed, I have had 17 different name changes. The perpetrator said he would kill us all, and I wanted to avoid him tracking me down.' Even Brad has had 14 name changes.

We lose our friends each time we change identities and move on. It is incredibly hard: you get to know a few people and get really friendly, and then you have to leave them behind. Only a couple of friends, who are like brothers and sisters to us – ever know who or where we are at any time.

Sometimes trying to remember their current identities can be very confusing.

I've been known as Tony, Christian, Christopher, Cameron . . . there's even a reference to me in one of the *Underbelly* shows under one of the names I went by for a while. Mixing with the *Underbelly* guys isn't something I'm proud of, but it was something I did to save my life at the time.

Follow the Money

In 1987, Chris got a job collecting money for a charity – rattling tins on street corners and encouraging people to give for a good cause. The problem was that although Chris, to this day, says he banked the money as ordered and that his superior siphoned off the funds, the charity and the courts begged to differ. He was sentenced to three years for embezzlement, with a non-parole period of two years. And that's when his real career in crime started. 'I was only 20 and there I was, in the Melbourne Remand Centre with guys like Peter Gibb (see chapter 5) and Nikolai Radev (see chapter 7). Of course, my life was going to change after that experience.' Peter Gibb and his lover, the prison officer Heather Parker, were both kind to the new inmate.

> And I knew full well what was going on between them. Peter Gibb was in the cell near the washing machines, then there was Nikolai Radev's cell, and then there was me. Me and Nik knew exactly what was going on because you could hear them in Gibb's cell at night when Heather was on duty. She was a nice lady, but her husband [another prison officer] was a really nasty man. Heather was very young and enthusiastic. For her, it was all about rehabilitating prisoners; he wanted to hang people for having a cigarette at the wrong time.

But it was Radev who really took the youngster under his wing. Chris, still searching for a father figure, lapped it up. 'You're put in with all those people and taught a code of conduct. If you breach it, you are in awful trouble.' But while Radev was supportive, he and his mates were also making good use of Chris's uncanny ability to spot a winner at the races.

> I used to study the form guide and get a couple of cans of Coke or something for my tips. One night, my tips got a bloke a trifecta that got him $14,000; another guy cleaned up four grand. Giving good tips became my protection. No-one was ever allowed to come near me after that.

Although he'd had a couple of experimental homosexual flings, Chris was not in a long-term relationship the first time he went to prison. Now – with the benefit of experience – he thinks that it is actually easier being single inside. 'When you have a partner on the outside, you're always concerned about their welfare, what they are up to, whether they are okay . . . When you're by yourself, there's no one to worry about but yourself.'

Which is not to say that there was no sex in prison.

I had sex more than once while I was in jail. Luckily, I was a big guy, so it was never forced on me, but it is different for the younger, smaller ones. Oral sex, in particular, can become an issue. I've definitely seen some young guys forced into things against their wills. They were told that if they didn't go along with it, either they or their families would be harmed.

Prison officers not only turned a blind eye, at times they even encouraged it, much to Chris's disgust.

At one prison, during my second sentence, the officers used to allow one [older] guy I knew to cross to a different part of the prison to have sex with a young fellow before everyone else had been let out of their cells. I'd started out being good friends with the older guy, but we ended up as good enemies. He wanted to kill me.

Chris can only think that the older guy must have had some kind of hold on the prison officers. 'And the young kid was supposedly in protection – so where was he meant to go for help? It was shocking, absolutely shocking.'

By the time Chris was released the first time, he was in tight with Radev's crew. He lapped up the feeling of belonging somewhere – along with the drugs that Radev supplied.

I used speed for six years after meeting Radev. He initially gave it to me because he thought I needed to lose some weight, and then I was hooked.

Chris never paid a cent for the drugs in all those years, but he was expected to help out in other ways – getting approved credit cards and the like.

> To the world, Radev may seem like an extremely bad criminal, but he wasn't a bad bloke. If I didn't have Christianity behind me, I'd probably be a much worse person too. I don't consider that running in on drug dealers and taking their drugs and money is such a bad thing anyway.

But his memories from that time aren't all good.

> I've seen people being given 'hot shots' [drugs laced with poison] in toilet blocks. I saw one bloke drowned in a living room in front of my eyes. I've seen things that no person should ever have to see. And it's all because they don't separate out violent criminals from non-violent criminals. If they did that, as someone in prison for a money crime, I would never have met those people. Do you know how many nightmares I've had ever since?

The life of crime is a risk to life as well to the chances of a good night's sleep, Chris reckons. 'Of those who were in Unit 5 at the Melbourne Remand Centre with me – Parker, Radev and the rest – basically only three or four of us are still alive.'

Two Peas in a Pod

By the early 1990s, Chris was working in Thailand and in a long-term relationship with another Australian, Jason, a heroin addict. 'It was a very violent relationship: one day he threatened me with a knife, so I picked up a wooden balcony chair and hit him over the head with it.' Thinking he'd killed his partner, Chris fled by boat and then train to Bangkok and made his way to the airport. 'It turned out Jason had only been knocked out. He found me at the airport and apologised, but it was too late.'

Chris flew to Sydney and settled in the suburb of Leichardt, but then decided to return to Thailand. 'I advertised in the paper for someone to look after my house and along comes Bradley – a wet-eared, wet-eyed 18-year-old who had nowhere to live.'

Their first contact did not begin well. 'When he rang about the ad, he was calling long distance from the country, and he kept running out of coins for the phone. I nearly just told him to forget about it, but I wouldn't trade him for all the tea in China now!'

The pair arranged to meet at Sydney's Central Station, and discussed the house-sitting arrangement over a few beers and then dinner. 'Brad confessed that he thought he was bisexual – the poor misguided brother!' Then the two went back to Chris's house. Brad played on the Playstation for a while, and then slept the night on the couch. Chris was still not keen on leaving the youngster in charge of the house and all his belongings. 'In fact, I couldn't stand the sight of him at the start. I nicknamed him The Lizard, because if you looked at the back of his neck, it was all red and scaly like a lizard. We often joke about that today.'

They also joke about how odd it was that they'd never met before Brad answered Chris's ad. Chris used to work in his spare time cooking at various missions for homeless people, and there was every chance that he'd cooked a meal for Brad one night. 'He thought he'd seen me about, but I can't remember it', says Chris.

The next morning after their rendezvous at Central Station, Chris woke up to find that there was a family crisis in another state. 'I told Brad that I wasn't prepared to let him house-sit, but that if he wanted to come on a road trip with me, he'd be welcome. I can't believe that he said he would, given that I was a person he'd only just met. Talk about risky.'

On that road trip, Brad somehow managed to crash the car. Chris told him: 'That car cost me three grand, so now you're going to stick around and work your debt off'. They are still together 19 years later. Last November, Brad stacked a car worth $35,000. 'You've got me for eternity now!' Brad told Chris.

In reality, the two didn't become a couple for about six months. While he'd been initially uninterested, slowly 'The Lizard' grew on Chris. 'We were on the road for a lot of that time, and one day I discovered Brad was epileptic. He was going to put our stuff in the car, and next thing I know I heard a thud and there he was on the floor, thrashing around. He'd wet himself too.'

Chris also began helping Brad out financially.

He only had one set of clothes with him, and there he was washing them day in day out. So I bought him some new clothes. One thing led to another and after about six months, we started going out. That was Melbourne Cup Day, 1993. I definitely know that he's the man for me, because we are two peas in a pod.

Separated by Bars

By choice, the two would never have been separated, but then Chris was arrested on more charges of embezzlement – almost a million dollars this time – and was back behind bars, leaving Brad alone on the outside.

'I served my second sentence in 2001 for credit card fraud – three years with a non-parole period of 18 months. That second sentence was awfully difficult. Brad stayed with my parents and went through every drug known to man because he wasn't coping without me', says Chris. Not even Brad's visits to Chris in jail could provide much solace.

'Brad and I were warned that because there were children around, if we kissed or cuddled, our visits would be cancelled immediately, and I'd be taken to the isolation unit. That was back in 2001, but it's not even allowed now, in 2012, when they're talking about gay marriage!'

Chris found it insulting that although same-sex couples are perfectly free to hold hands or show affection out on the street, he and his partner were not allowed to touch or kiss at all in the prison visiting room.

And it's not as though we're going to be doing it for two hours straight – so to speak. I'm talking about giving him a hug or a kiss hello and goodbye, or to sit there holding hands to give each other strength . . . you know, to encourage each other not to give up. It was unfair and very hurtful.

During Chris's first sentence, he had hidden the fact that he was gay. 'I hid it very well, even to the point where some of my mates, as a bit of a joke, used to hold me down and give me love bites so that the prison officers would think I was gay. They didn't realise that I really was!'

Throughout his second sentence, and now partnered with Brad, he decided that there was no point in maintaining the façade.

I ran into some of my mates from the previous time and when I told them, they said, 'You're gay? What about when we gave you those love bites?' And I said, 'Yeah well, I fancied you, didn't I?' That shocked the pants off them. They certainly didn't want to give me any more love bites after that!

Chris never encountered any particular problems after coming out in prison. One of his best mates (also known as his 'Five Eight' – rhymes with 'mate') was straight.

We used to share a cell and it was always a bit of a joke between us. One time, my mate had some problems and I went and sorted them out for him. That night, he started calling out my name in his sleep – calling out so loudly that he woke himself up. 'See, you do fancy me!' I told him.

The prison officers would sometimes stir up trouble, often to suit their own ends. Chris still blames one for planting a homemade knife, known as a 'shiv', in his cell. 'Then of course he found it when he searched my cell and I was charged. You can't argue back, because who are the authorities going to believe: a crim like me or an officer? You just have to accept the penalty and tough titties if you don't like it.' After the knife was found, Chris was moved to another prison – the whole point of the exercise, according to a friendlier officer at Chris's new prison, who said that the old shiv trick was often used as an excuse for moving inmates around.

Together, Inside

When Chris met Brad, Brad had never been inside an adult prison – he was barely an adult – so seven years later he was lucky that he had the more experienced Chris (his partner to boot) alongside him for his first taste of life behind bars. 'It was actually a bit ridiculous. We'd headed from Perth to South Australia in a rental car and were arrested at the border for stealing it. The payment had cleared on the credit card, so we had no idea what they were on about', explains Chris. It turned out that the problem lay in taking the car across the state border – something they hadn't declared they'd be doing to the rental company. The two were thrown – together – into Port Augusta prison for six days until the issue was finally sorted it out.

Brad was really scared, because this was back in the 1990s, and the prison was very basic: no TV, communal showers, that kind of thing. I kept telling him that it would be OK, and trying to make him feel comfortable, but he was terrified. He was also sure that I was going to be extradited to Victoria and he'd be left there alone to face the music.

At the time Chris was wanted in Victoria for another crime, but the South Australian police released him once the car issue had been clarified . . . much to the annoyance of the Victorians. Chris has tried to keep on the right side of the law ever since.

When it comes to prison, I've been there, done that, and don't want to do it again. I've also been blessed by having good friends who've pushed me onto the straight and narrow. For the past 10 or 11 years, I've kept myself mostly crime free and totally free of all drugs, alcohol or other addictions. All I want to do is keep my nose clean and to be left alone.

Brad, though, has not been so fortunate, and Chris today often finds himself on the other side of the prison bars, visiting his partner.

The Snap

Brad's crime isn't embezzlement or violence or drug dealing or theft, but drug addiction, as Chris sees it. In fact, Chris doesn't consider Brad a criminal, but a man with a medical problem.

For Brad to smoke a bit of pot, and for people to condemn him for it, well – if other people had his background, they'd be on heroin or worse. He was 37 years old, had never been in trouble, even for a driving offence, and then all of a sudden one day he snapped.

It's not as if Brad didn't recognise that he had a problem. He'd even been to see a drug and alcohol counsellor, but he found that resources were tight and getting access to a detox centre would be tough, even for someone with top-level medical cover, as Brad had. 'The counsellor Brad saw said that there was little she could do, that there was a long wait for drug rehab and that it would require lots of money.'

Brad's real problems began two weeks later when he had an episode of drug-induced psychosis, possibly caused by the combination of the methamphetamine and marijuana he'd started to take. At home with him at the time, Chris (who's stayed clear of drugs for years now) says that Brad simply went nuts. Then he took off in their car (the $35,000 car that Brad will be paying off for eternity). Realising that something was seriously amiss, Chris rang the police and alerted them that Brad, at this moment, was a danger both to himself and possibly to others. Chris and another friend, Luke, took off in pursuit. Luke describes a very fraught situation:

> By then, the police had gathered out the front of the local store in the town that we lived in. We pulled up next to the police cars and Chris told the sergeant in charge that he thought Brad was psychotic and that if they chased him, he was likely to crash his car on purpose. We heard the sergeant yelling into his radio 'Do not chase! Do not chase!' but one patrol car ignored him. Two seconds later, Brad crashed his car.

Chris describes it as the most frightening moment of his life. 'The car was totalled, but the only thing that wasn't damaged or obliterated was the driver's seat. He was a very, very, VERY lucky boy.' Brad managed to work himself free and, still obviously under the influence of drugs, was tackled by police. 'He was tasered, they used up three capsicum sprays on him, and still he didn't go down.

In the end, it took about five policemen to get him under control. If that's not proof that he was having a psychotic episode, I don't know what they need.'

What happened next is what still upsets Chris. Brad was taken by Medivac to the hospital in the closest major city, his home town not having the resources to deal with him at that point, and the Royal Flying Doctor Service refusing to fly such a dangerous criminal.

When Chris finally showed up at the hospital, after a long night's drive, he entered the Emergency Department to find Brad chained to the bed with four sets of handcuffs, and four policemen guarding him. Chris was outraged on a number of accounts:

First, they had withheld Brad's essential epilepsy medication. Second, as Brad had already been sectioned under the Mental Health Act, no police should have been allowed to have been present, in case Brad said something detrimental to his case. Besides, he'd been given so much sedative that to this day he can't remember much about it. I don't know what they thought he was going to do. Yes, what he had done in crashing the car and resisting arrest was wrong, but he was mentally ill at the time. It was like they didn't want him to be on Earth any more, but to go somewhere else.

When Chris first walked into Brad's room and heard the policemen taunting the shackled prisoner, the policemen initially thought he was a nurse and asked what the hell Chris thought he was doing. 'I said that I was Brad's *partner*, not a nurse, and that they had no right to treat him this way.'

None of Chris's complaints about the way Brad was treated after his arrest (he reckons there were 153 abuses of Brad's rights) has been officially upheld, although some people in authority have expressed sympathy in private, says Chris. On public record is the fact that Brad was eventually sentenced for 12 months for the assault of five police officers. He was told at sentencing that he would be sent to a mental health facility where he would get the help he so clearly needed, but instead Brad found himself inside the state's main prison.

'He was told that if he acted up, he'd be sent to the toughest part of the prison', says Chris. 'So to calm himself down, at what was a very stressful time, he turned straight back to marijuana, of course.'

Send Lawyers, Drugs and Money

'The hardest part of Brad going to jail was knowing what he was going through. He's an epileptic, he had psych problems, and I knew that prison was not helping him. I'd just go to bed every night and cry', says Chris. 'The only respite he had in there was marijuana.'

It was an expensive form of respite. 'Just half a gram – not an ounce, but a gram – could cost $100 inside. That was hugely more expensive than on the outside.'

Those on the inside, discovering Brad's weakness for pot and that he had a loving partner, were only all too ready to leverage the opportunity. Chris says that while Brad was in the main prison, they were blackmailed into helping get marijuana inside. It's not something that Chris is proud of, but he says he had no choice.

There are some tough guys in there on long sentences and when they say, 'Bring the stuff in or else', you know they mean business. One guy was doing a very long time on a murder sentence; another was a major drug dealer. What was I meant to say? If I'd said no, I knew that they had access to and could hurt my partner. They threatened to kill him, and I needed to protect Brad at all costs.

Despite never having had a drug conviction in his life, Chris was soon a regular buyer. At one stage, he was arranging for marijuana to be delivered every few days to a contact on the outside, who would then arrange for it to make its way into the prison past the eyes of the guards. One quarter would go to Brad – the rest would be sold to other inmates.

I often wonder if there is someone in the administration who has an interest in the trade continuing. You can't tell me that the officers don't know what is going on. I've visited prison so many times, and they way they scrutinise you going in, I'd never be game to try to smuggle in drugs. I've been told they get women to bring it in in their bra, made up in tiny packets with little water balloons. During a visit, the women somehow get them out and hand them over to the blokes. Then the blokes swallow the balloons and regurgitate them later when they're back in their cell. The whole thing is ludicrous.

It was also illegal and exorbitantly expensive. The cost to Chris over just one year was around $100,000 – a huge amount for anyone, let alone a small-business owner. At the end of that time, he was living hand to mouth and grateful that the bank had not foreclosed on his house.

Eventually Brad was told that he would be moving to a prison closer to home – a blessing for Chris, who'd spent hours each weekend driving to visit Brad, only to be allowed half an hour or so. But just 16 days before Brad's transfer to the local prison, he was moved from minimum to maximum security. Here he was severely beaten – a final standover attempt to extort more money, Chris believes, before Brad was shipped out to his local prison.

Neighbourhood Watch

Chris had high hopes before he moved to the regional hub where he and Brad set up their home and business – well before the incident when Brad went crazy on meth and pot, and was sent to prison. But Chris's own record had been enough to set off alarms at the local police station. The local coppers were among the first to knock on the door after their arrival. 'They just turned up on our doorstep and said that people like me weren't welcome in the area. I told them that I just wanted a quiet life, and that I hadn't been in trouble in years.' It wasn't a great start to their new life.

> I think the gay thing is a huge thing in this state. Some of the police here have called me a fag and a poof, and told me that people like me should be put to death. And that is the police! If I am in trouble, what am I meant to do – go to the police when they treat me like that? I think they'd love to see me go off the rails and go back to prison.

Or perhaps to the morgue.

> I have never been convicted of a violent crime in my life, but the local police have told me that if I ever have to call for an ambulance, it will be accompanied by two police cars. They've told me that they won't bother rushing either.

It's not the same in other states, believes Chris.

> I know a lot of other police officers in Tasmania, for example, who respect what I'm trying to do and know I want to go straight. They are behind me. Tassie is the best place in the world . . . they don't judge you, and they don't give you a hard time. Sure, if you

commit a crime, you can expect a punishment, but if you don't, then you can expect a normal life in the community.

Grudgingly, Chris admits that a few of the local policemen and policewomen are OK. 'The last time Brad broke parole – they found out he'd been using drugs again from his regular urine analysis – they rang and said that they'd be there in 15 minutes, and to be ready to go back to prison. He was fine with that.'

It was rather different the first time Brad had a bad drug result after his release from prison on parole.

Instead of just meeting him at the parole office and saying, 'Come on sunshine, you're under arrest', they blocked the area off and arrested him in the street outside with nine police officers and three detectives. I was beside myself. I didn't know how he'd react to that. You'd have thought he was Al Capone from all the fuss they made.

Love Has No Limits

After Brad's treatment during his breakdown and their subsequent experiences, Chris has written too many letters to be able to count.

The only person I haven't written to yet is the prime minister and she is next on the list. Yes, Brad did the crime of assaulting police officers and has to do the time. But is prison meant to be about punishment or rehabilitation? Whenever he comes out, his drug reading is higher than it ever is on the outside.

On leaving jail, one of Brad's blood readings gave a level of 0.978 for THC, one of the key components of marijuana. Registering a relatively low 0.165 one week while on the outside was enough to breach the conditions of his parole and land him back inside.

Are they serious? I know that Brad has a problem with pot, but how does putting him back inside help with making him better or preventing him from re-offending. Where is the rehabilitation? They should be doing something in there to help him, not making him worse. Not giving him access to even more drugs.

Obviously, Chris says, this is something that the prison system doesn't want to be made public.

The whole thing smells of corruption, and I don't care if someone is the Queen of England, if they are corrupt or hurt my partner, I am going to work to bring them down. You'd understand locking him up if they were also rehabilitating him. But for God's sake, give the prisoners a goal in life; don't just lock them up for a trivial thing like smoking pot, when they are doing the best they can. People say it is his choice to take drugs, but it is not. It is an illness. Would you put a needle in your arm or whatever if you knew that you were going to be tested and the results meant you were going back to prison? If that doesn't prove Brad is an addict, then I don't know what would. Put him in a detox unit, not a prison.

Chris points out that if civilians – that is, non-criminals – were to be caught with a gram of marijuana, most policemen would probably look the other way. 'But when it comes to Brad, someone who has a real problem, for him to have one or two cones to settle his nerves after all he has been through is considered a jailable offence. That is just plain wrong.'

Drugs are particularly rife in the regional town where Chris and Brad decided to make their home. And that's something he'd like to see changed.

I've been to the police a dozen times about guys round here selling drugs, but nothing ever happens. I've even offered to go and buy drugs under surveillance to help clean the area up, but they said they couldn't risk my life like that. My response was: 'But you are willing to risk the life of my partner?' And if Brad continues with drugs, who knows what will happen?

Carer and Carer

On paper, Brad may present as a cop beater, a druggie with a violent bent, but Chris says that it couldn't be further from the truth. Normally, he's just a regular guy at home – looking after Chris and their dogs, playing computer games or perhaps a game of Texas hold 'em poker with their few local friends. That time he snapped is the only time he has done so.

Whenever they are apart, Brad worries about Chris, and about his health. Chris had a heart attack in 2012 – partly brought on by the stress of the previous two years, he thinks.

When Brad is out of jail, if I'm crook, he'll say anything to keep me calm so my heart rate doesn't go up. But if I'm well, then look out! He'll tell me what it is all about and what I have done wrong. It's annoying at times, but I wouldn't swap him for anything.

Whenever Brad returns to jail for another parole violation for using drugs, he's not the only one being punished.

I'm on a pension now that we've given up the business and Brad has been on a pension to care for me. When he goes to prison, I still have to pay all the same bills, but on half the money. I also have to pay for him while he is in jail, and if he doesn't have money to call me that stresses me out too. Meanwhile I have no-one to look after me, and I go without so that I can give money to him in there.

They took no compassion on us, even knowing that Brad is my carer. They told me that when he was in prison, if I couldn't cope, that I'd have to go into residential care. But what happens to our house, our dogs, our lives, then? I was fortunate that I had one friend, Luke, who has been prepared to help me out for free. He is a godsend. You really work out who your friends are when your partner is in jail. Most of this community has completely ostracised us.

Luke is actually an ex-partner of Chris's – from a time when Chris and Brad were briefly apart. Now Chris is back with Brad, and Luke is a permanent fixture in their lives. He's the closest thing to a best friend for both them. Surprisingly, given the tangled relationship history, Brad and Luke get on really well. 'Without Luke's support while Brad has been inside, I don't think I would have made it this far', says Chris.

At the time of writing, Brad had broken parole and left the state, not wanting to return to prison after yet another failed drug test. Chris is standing by his man. 'You don't just walk away from a relationship. I believe in the truth of the traditional marriage vows – the whole bit about loving someone in sickness and in health, and no matter what happens.'

However, marriage is not on the cards:

I believe that God created Adam and Eve, not Adam and Steve. Children are the whole point of marriage, and as Brad and I clearly can't produce children, I don't believe that we should be able to get married. I also believe that homosexuality is a sin, but it is my sin and I have to carry it.

Going Straight

Chris is firmly committed to Brad and their future together.

We've been together 19 years now and we've lasted three sentences during that time – one of mine, one of his and one together. Him skipping out on parole is just another blip. It is only our strength and love for each other that has gotten us through. Nothing else could have conquered the time apart, the distance, the threats, the stress or the violence we've experienced, but love.

Chapter 10
Love You a Legend

The lyrics to the song 'The Impossible Dream' hold a special resonance for Carolyn Wilkinson, astrologer, mother and long-term partner of Daniel Heiss – a man who at one time was the target of the biggest manhunt ever seen in the Northern Territory. It is a song of hope, with lyrics that talk about loving someone from a distance, bearing sorrow, righting wrongs and striving for the 'unreachable star' even when weary from the struggle. 'In hindsight, the song described our situation perfectly. And with the way it talks about the stars, it was written for me, I'm sure of it.'

The song was written for the 1965 musical, *Man of La Mancha*, and describes Don Quixote's impossible quest. Carolyn too, knows what it is like 'to tilt at windmills'. She spent years supporting Heiss in prison, campaigning for prison reforms to make Northern Territory's prisons, if not bearable, at least liveable, and also advocating for Heiss's parole against a system that was seemingly determined to keep him inside indefinitely. He'd been given a life sentence for murder in the one place in Australia where life really does mean life.

Daniel Luther Heiss and Peter Michael Kamm were charged with murder after the death of Peter Dean Robinson, aged 22, on a hunting trip. The evidence presented to the court was that Kamm had fired the shots that killed the young man, and that Heiss had helped Kamm dispose of the body.

Heiss was just 25 years old in January 1991 when a Northern Territory Supreme Court jury found him guilty of Robinson's murder – or murder by derivative liability, to be more legally precise. In other words, Heiss hadn't fired the fatal shot or shots, but had been there and done nothing to prevent Robinson's death. He was guilty by association.

The judge sentenced Heiss to life imprisonment, with the recommendation that he serve at least 10 years for his part in the offence. It had been shown in court that his actions had not been the cause of Robinson's death, he had no prior criminal convictions and he had a clean record aside from some traffic infringements and a parking fine. His parents were advised that he might be out within seven years, with any luck, if he behaved well inside.

But the timing couldn't have been worse. Not long after Heiss had been sentenced, and after some secretive politicking at the highest levels, the government introduced a 20-year mandatory sentence for murder, to be applied retrospectively to all lifers in the territory's prison system – Heiss now among them. There would be no chance of the Parole Board even looking at a particular case until 20 years had been served behind bars. Heiss's sentence was literally doubled overnight, and even then he'd still have to await the Parole Board's approval for release. And the old rule of time off for good behaviour had been scrapped too.

The changes to the law made a media splash at the time, but Carolyn Wilkinson didn't pay much attention. She was busy working, bringing up two young children and battling through the last days of a long-term relationship that was on the verge of collapse. With the sweeping changes to the law and looking down the barrel of at least a couple of decades inside, Heiss now considered he had nothing to lose. He began plotting his escape. He knew as an escapee that he'd be looking down the barrel of a gun instead, but anything had to be better than prison.

His first successful attempt at flight from the Berrimah maximum-security prison was in 1991. Heiss had engineered a trip to hospital by faking a ruptured peptic ulcer, and it was from the fourth floor of the Royal Darwin Hospital that he actually made his escape. This he did by knotting together all the sheets and towels and electrical cords he could find into a homemade rope, then smashing out the window with a heavy steel cabinet and lowering himself the four floors to the ground. He was picked up by police a couple of days later, having been spotted emerging from a mangrove swamp, covered in mud, to cross a road.

Carolyn Wilkinson didn't register the news of his escape; nor did she notice when the papers announced that Daniel Heiss, convicted killer, was back behind bars again. But his next escape would both gain her attention and change both their lives.

Into the Unknown

The next time Heiss escaped, it was over the razor wire of Berrimah maximum-security prison itself, in the company of another lifer, Shane Baker, who was also in prison for murder. Given the changes in the law, and the length of the sentence both men were facing, they were prepared to risk all for freedom, rather than 'live a life inside without hope', as Carolyn describes it.

The escape had been planned for months, and involved the painstaking creation of a key – each notch copied from the memory of seeing a prison officer's master key. Heiss and Baker created their version out of metal using miniature files, and then fine tuned its exact form through secret practise on various doors. Bizarrely enough, the homemade key worked, allowing the men out of their cells and into the yard, where they then scaled a number of razor-wire fences.

In her searing book of Heiss's experiences, *Blood on the Wire*, self-published in 2012, Carolyn Wilkinson describes the atmosphere in Darwin at the time of Heiss and Baker's escape. She and her family were living in the area where the two prisoners were thought to be hiding out:

The heady scent of jasmine hung in the air. If I wanted, I could slice the air into neat squares and squeeze a bucket of water from each one. I wanted it to rain. Everyone did. Maybe if it rained properly those bloody choppers would stop their incessant hammering.

I looked up as one of the helicopters banked deeply and thundered away. Time to refuel. The second chopper would soon follow. If I could see the pattern, that poor bastard out there certainly could too. None too bright, some of those coppers – unless it was part of the plan to fool him into thinking the coast was clear. I shrugged, and turned back into the kitchen, letting the screen door close gently behind me.

I had plenty to do – sort out the kids and get started on the housework. I should have done the laundry earlier, in the cool, but I'd been listening to the radio, distracted by the drama that was intensifying out there in the scrub.

Something made me uneasy. I'd felt it for days. It wasn't fear. I'd never felt scared for myself or my children, even when encountering roadblocks a few days back. And then the news: two convicted killers had escaped from Berrimah prison. Do not approach the 'dangerous' bastards. There were rumours of a shoot-to-kill order, and I didn't like it.

As the facts began to emerge, I felt a shift in the mood in Howard Springs. No longer would two hardened criminals slaughter us all in our beds. Sightings went unreported; food was left out, along with clothing and cash. And when the first of the fugitives was captured without a fight, barely walking and in terrible pain, we began to ask what was really happening. Why would someone want to put themselves through such suffering and deprivation in one of the most inhospitable environments in the world? It made me wonder. What would drive someone to go to the trouble of escaping, let alone giving up three square meals a day and a dry mattress, to place themselves squarely at the wrong end of a gun barrel?

Something was beginning to smell. And the jasmine couldn't hide it.

Carolyn had spent much of her youth and young adulthood studying everything from tarot to reiki, psychic healing, earth changes, crystals and flower remedies. She was fascinated by mythology, crop circles, and the idea of destiny. In her mid-twenties, astrology became her passion. With Heiss on the run in her own neighbourhood, it was a natural thing for Carolyn to consider what the stars had in store for him.

I hadn't been worried by the idea that there were two 'dangerous' men hiding out near our home, strangely enough. I just had the feeling that he wasn't going to hurt anyone. What Daniel had done – escaping from prison – was pretty full on and I wondered what had driven him to do it. I wondered what stars he had, and what was in his charts for the future. When I read his charts, my jaw dropped. He had a pretty dramatic horoscope.

And the next 12 days were to prove very dramatic, even if Carolyn didn't know the full details until much later. Heiss and Baker were being hunted by the largest taskforce ever to be assembled in the Northern Territory – more than 200 policemen, helicopters, Aboriginal trackers, dog squads . . . Over 11 long days and nights, the pair eluded capture. Along the way they dodged croc-infested creeks, suffered wild hallucinations and violent cramps from unfamiliar bush foods, and escaped numerous close shaves with their pursuers. For much of the time, they were hungry and thirsty, and sore. Baker had torn his leg badly on the last roll of razor wire during their escape; Heiss had to deal with the indignity and pain of a centipede bite on the tip of his penis. Not to mention the swarming march flies, mozzies and biting ants . . .

Eventually the pair was caught – Baker first, thanks to his injured leg, then Heiss. Both were returned to prison.

Carolyn was still intrigued by the escape, and was determined to do Heiss's astrological chart.

Daniel's police mug shot had been plastered all over the place during the escape, but I couldn't make out his birth date, so I decided to write to him and find out exactly when and where he was born. Getting in touch with him was totally astrologically motivated – it certainly wasn't his mug shot, which wasn't flattering at all!

As Carolyn describes it, she felt compelled by some force to write that first letter to Heiss. 'I'm not the stereotypical person who'd just write to a prisoner out of the blue, but I felt deep inside me that it was something I just had to do. So I did.' The letter began: 'Dear Mr Heiss, I'm a student of astrology and may be able to assist you in some form or manner. But, to do this, I need your birth date, time and place . . .' She signed it simply, The Astrologer.

'By then, I had just broken up from my other relationship, I had kids to look after and I wasn't looking for anything more than to do his chart.' Besides, Carolyn says that she recognised that he was in a vulnerable situation, and she didn't want to lead him on.

Several weeks later came the reply from Heiss, who'd been waiting to hear back from his mother about the exact time of his birth. He addressed her simply as Dear Astrologer, and expressed an abiding fascination in mysticism, which only served to pique her interest further. She prepared a full astrological chart for him. 'She had a pretty good handle on me right away!' he says. 'She also gave me knowledge about myself that I couldn't get any other way at that time. It was like a mirror for me to have a good look at myself.'

In one of his letters, included in *Blood on the Wire*, he explained to her why he had escaped:

I found out that they changed my sentence. What was the point of staying? I could have stayed put, doing it easy with my painting and my hobby and working out, but in jail you can feel yourself dying, rotting, with a psychological yoke around your neck. Knives are sharpened on a stone. Men are sharpened on each other.

Heiss describes the period of time after his recapture as the absolute end of the road. 'I had nothing left inside. It's like if you try to climb a mountain and don't make it, you don't feel like doing anything else. Then Carolyn wrote to me and got me back on track.'

The two shared an interest in astrology and music, mystical matters, meditation, the Dreamtime, the natural environment and art – both Heiss and Carolyn's favourite subject at school. But for a long time, around six months, Heiss didn't even know if she was male or female, old or young. 'That did my head in for a while', he says. He was definitely curious, but Carolyn avoided the topic, saying:

> Now, I must tell you in all honesty, I have not ignored your more personal questions. Let me put it this way: when you need to write to a bloke, write to me. And when you need to write to a woman, write to me. I seek to heal not harm, that is all.

The pesky question of her sex put aside, their friendship continued to develop through an increasingly steady stream of letters. 'We had a weird connection even though we'd never met at that stage, and somehow I could sense him holding his breath. I consider the breath to be the soul or life's force, and it was like he wasn't really living. I just wanted him to breathe.' She wrote this to him:

> You need to do the work because I can't do it for you. There's no quick fix. My time is precious in my life, Daniel. I'm willing to help you, but you must make the effort to help yourself. I think we can do much. You have the time to help yourself, to regenerate, and breathe. Please stop holding your breath. Remember to breathe.

Looking back now, after so many years together, Carolyn is surprised at how quickly they opened up to each other. 'It was like we already knew each other. I read my letters to him now, and think, '"Did I really say that?"' Sometimes Heiss's letters took on an abrupt or defensive tone, but Carolyn took it all in her stride. 'I think much of that had to do with the environment he was living in. It must have been hard to get out of that head space to write to me. Also, I was a stranger at first – I could have been anyone.'

Heiss found Carolyn's forthright nature appealing. But he admits that she is not so great to argue with.

With the astrology, one time I found some discrepancies between what she'd told me earlier and what she was telling me now. I like a bit of a debate, so I asked her about it and her reply was, 'Oh, astrology's not static – it's fluid!' So much for a good debate!

At the time Heiss was actually seeing another woman – if 'seeing' is the right term for a relationship conducted mainly in prison waiting rooms. Bizarrely enough, Kelly was a policewoman, who'd first seen Heiss at the time of his arrest after escaping and had then pursued further contact – without letting on that she was a copper, naturally enough. Instead, Kelly had claimed to be a DJ, but Heiss found out her real career later when a trusted mate blew the whistle on her. When Carolyn and Heiss began their correspondence, Kelly was helping to organise an exhibition of his artworks on the outside.

Heiss was clearly a magnetic character and very attractive to women. The description of 'womaniser' is one that Heiss admits hearing many times in his youth. And not even prison bars could keep the admirers away. Inspired by his escape and the coverage in the press, many other strangers – male and female – wrote to him too, sometimes with graphic sexual detail. One particularly fervent admirer, Flame, wasn't fussy about whom she wrote to. A friend of Heiss saw her advertisement in a magazine asking to meet some bikers!

Writing to prisoners is a well-known phenomenon, but it still surprised Heiss, who'd had little outside attention from anyone before his escape. 'When you've escaped and you are also a convicted murderer, it's like there is some bubble around you. People would project their own stuff onto me – some wanted to save my soul, some wanted to have sex with me. Carolyn wanted to help me.'

Some women might have been put off by the fact that there were other women on the scene, but Carolyn was secure in their friendship and open to more. 'I hadn't told him anything about how my feelings for him had started to change or the dreams I had about him, and I wasn't going to. I couldn't promise anything at that stage. I thought maybe it wasn't real – maybe it would just go away.'

Heiss's art had long fascinated Carolyn too; the envelopes he sent her were often intricately drawn on and coloured, and often there were little sketches or drawings inside. Before she'd even met him, she went along to his first exhibition, *Eye of the Wind*, held at the Studio Star Gallery in Darwin, which was a runaway success. What really blew her away was how much of what they'd discussed in their letters had turned up in his art. The importance of breathing, the planets, landscapes, his stars . . . some of his dreams that he'd discussed with her. Since then, Heiss has had a number of solo exhibitions: *Hand of Fire* (Darwin), *Heart of Gold* (Sydney), *Awaken* (Sydney) and *Belly of Clay* (Darwin), *Will of Freedom* at the Darwin Entertainment Centre, and *Continuum* at the Artwarehouse in Darwin.

They didn't meet until nearly a year after Carolyn wrote that first letter, and her first sight of Heiss in the flesh was not auspicious. Ushered into the waiting room, Carolyn was greeted by the sight of his bare bum poking up in the air as he struggled to get into the regulation red overalls that all prisoners were forced to wear when meeting visitors. Only when he finally turned around did she notice his eyes – deep green – and his Cheshire cat smile.

Today, Heiss says that at that time he was probably already half in love.

I think I fell in love with her mind before I'd even met her. I'd had an image of her in my mind as kind of bird-like, kind of thin and intellectual. Or maybe a bit of a hippy. And she's not like either of them. She has her own style. And I was surprised because she has very strong hands and very strong shoulders too. She had strength and she was beautiful.

But Heiss was still seeing Kelly. It looked like Carolyn and Heiss's friendship was going to stay just that.

Love from Afar

Towards the end of 1996, Heiss was transferred to the Alice Springs Correctional Centre – lured there by promises from the administration that it was a new prison and that he'd have access to a pool, a gym and all kinds of goodies unknown in Darwin. It sounded too good to be true and when he arrived, he found out it was. The promised 'luxury facility' was just a ruse to ease overcrowding and convince prisoners to transfer. But Heiss had also been going stir crazy in Darwin. 'One day I went out into the yard and realised that there wasn't a single spot in the place where I hadn't already sat another day. I had to get out, otherwise I was going to go mad.'

In their first phone call after his transfer, Carolyn finally confessed to Heiss that she loved him. 'I'd loved him for a long time, but it wasn't until he was in Alice that I actually told him.'

His reply was immediate: 'Why didn't you bloody tell me? If I'd known, I would have stayed in Darwin!'

Heiss says that once they'd made the commitment to try and make their relationship work, he never had a moment's doubt about Carolyn.

I would never have become emotionally involved with her unless I'd known that I could put my eggs into her basket, so to speak. If you don't have a sense of security and trust in your partner, a man in prison can go crazy. And they do. But Carolyn is a very honest, straightforward person. I knew that if she met someone else then she would tell me first.

She continued to write with messages of love and hope.

You can cultivate gentleness, and you can develop humour, and you can find your own depth. Or you can stay in your shell, fighting in the dark. All things that grow are plunged into darkness – the seed in the soil and the baby in the womb. Our inner darkness is necessary to give us time for the release of growth and in the dark are the instructions for finding the light – in the tree is the seed, and in the baby is the man, in the grain of sand is the universe. And I do believe that when you turn that light on and find your full potential, you'll find yourself in a room full of gems with nothing broken.

The seed in the soil analogy resonated strongly with Heiss. 'Yes, I am a seed in the soil. I like that. All things that grow are plunged into darkness. This is me – in jail, in the dark like a mushroom.'

With Carolyn in Darwin and Heiss now in Alice Springs, visits were an expensive – and rare – luxury.

I got very little support from my family and friends. I lost a few friends when they found out I was with Daniel, but my true friends stuck by me. Daniel's parents were in Sydney and couldn't get there often, but they helped me out so I could see him once or twice a year. The first time I saw him down there, he looked like a different man. Pale, thin, like the wind had been knocked out of his sails . . . the prison down there was a complete hell-hole. I only ever visited him once in winter down there, because it was so cold. The prisoners had no warm clothes and he just sat there and shivered the whole time. I couldn't bear it. It was horrible. So I didn't go in winter again.

For much of the seven years he spent in the Alice Springs Correctional Centre, Heiss was in solitary confinement and maximum security – stuck in a tiny cell with a tiny yard, the roof of which was covered in wire mesh. For company, he had the occasional visiting bull ant, hordes of crows, and the ever-present dust. For a long time, he had no access to his art materials, or even to a phone for more than 10 minutes, once a month. It must have been unbearably lonely. He wrote to her: 'I see no-one. Not even crims. But, I don't mind, I'm a loner anyway. I'm so alone and I'm only human. I kiss your hands, and I kiss your lips. Love Daniel.'

'Our relationship was built on dreams, on poetry, on things we *could* share', says Heiss. The letters were an important part of it. 'When you're inside and people write to you, it takes over your world, because you're cut off from everything and everyone else.'

They developed many little rituals to bring them closer together when they were so far apart. 'We'd choose a song to listen to at the same time so we could tune into each other. Or we'd make a time where we would both sit down, charge a glass of water and drink a toast to each other', says Carolyn. 'Other times I'd make a meal for him and imagine him sitting down to eat it with me.' But she never told him about this private ceremony at the time. 'The food he had was so horrible, I could hardly tell him about the lovely steak I'd cooked him. That would have been torture – too cruel!'

Over time, the pair even developed their own language. 'Love you a legend' became their regular sign-off, begun by Carolyn.

I don't know where it came from; it just popped straight out of my head and onto the paper one day when I was finishing up a letter. Daniel picked up on it straight away. LYAL, we'd call it for short. One time I rang the prison psychologist in Alice to make sure that Dan was OK and asked her to pass on a message: 'Smile LYAL'. That was one of our little secret messages – there was also 'Kiss your cosmos', 'Hug your history', 'Trust me a mountain'. It was our language of love put into the letters. It's all we had.

Fearing that words such as LYAL might be code for a prison break or something equally sinister, eventually the prison censor sent the couple's letters back demanding an explanation. 'I had to send the man a legend so he could decipher our letters and see that we weren't up to anything', says Carolyn.

But it's tough surviving in a town like Alice, and even tougher keeping a relationship together over an extended time apart, Heiss explains:

Relationships with women when you're in jail are really just abstract. You have to find another outlet for the physical expression, and I put mine into my art. One time I drew some romantic pictures of us making love, and I was called in to see the Superintendent. He called them obscene, and wouldn't let me send them. The place is brutal like that.

The lack of physical contact is definitely an issue, says Heiss, and one that not only results in forced or unwilling sexual contact, particularly for younger inmates, but also in long-term homosexual relationships. 'Some guys who've been sharing a cell for years end up just like an old married couple. In an environment like prison, people think and behave differently to how they would on the outside.'

Heiss says that it was only the constant contact with women – his unknown letter writers, Kelly, and then Carolyn – 'that kept me from becoming a faggot. I kept my head focused on women the whole time. Having that outlet is important, as it stopped me from becoming full of bad passion. Carolyn really understood me as a man and my virility, and kept me going – literally for years.'

Psychologically, the prison in Alice was far tougher on Heiss than Darwin had ever been.

I was stuck in a little yard by myself for seven years. When I did leave and go into mainstream, I went into a yard with nearly 50 full-blood Aborigines and just one other white bloke. We used to walk out into the yard together every morning, for safety, and we always had to shade our eyes with our hats – you can't go looking at black fellas in the eyes too much down there as it is offensive to them.

The sheer number of indigenous inmates was difficult to come to terms with for Heiss, who admits that as a white Australian, it's easy to lead a life that is pretty much separate when you're not forced into close proximity through sharing a tiny space. Inside, he was continually confronted with aspects of a different culture, a different race. 'Everyone in prison has to find strength in their own identity to survive. That said, I've seen blokes in there who were white, but after a few years they were claiming to be black!'

Throughout it all, Heiss drew strength from his art, keeping fit and his love of Australia's history as a convict nation – it gave him heart that plenty of other blokes had been where he now was, and had survived. 'Most of all though, it was Carolyn who kept me sane. I think it was fate that she started writing to me.'

The Endless Struggle

For years, Heiss had been fighting for the chance to transfer to a prison near his family in New South Wales. But despite the Northern Territory being a signatory to legislation specifying that if a prisoner's welfare was at risk, he could be transferred to prison closer to his home, he'd been repeatedly knocked back.

Heiss's situation was highlighted in a story on the *7.30 Report* about the transfer of inmates between prisons. He'd served nearly 14 years already (enough to merit his release in practically any other jurisdiction in Australia except the Northern Territory).

Carolyn supported his request that he be moved interstate, worried by his continued isolation in Alice Springs, and the deterioration of his health. Even if it meant that he would be further away from her, she wanted whatever was best for him. She told the *7.30 Report* that with a transfer, she believed that his health would improve and that his family would be able to visit him often, instead of just once a year.

His parents made no comment to the program at the time; they were still in shock from losing their home and all their possessions – including a large collection of Heiss's prison artworks – during a major bushfire just before the program was broadcast.

Airing Heiss's plight on the ABC made no difference. His application for an interstate transfer continued to be rejected. Instead, Heiss managed to transfer back to Darwin in 2004, to be closer to Carolyn.

The one glimmer of hope they had at the time came from the introduction, in 2002, of the Parole Reform Bill. This was designed to give those convicted of 'aggravated murder' an extra five-year non-parole period – raising it from 20 to 25 years. Carolyn had even gone along to parliament to see the legislation being brought in.

The Act was designed as extra punishment for mass murderers or those who'd killed a child or a policeman, but none of those applied to Daniel's case. It sounds dreadful to describe his case as a 'standard' murder, but that's how it was considered under the new Act. It now looked like he would be eligible for parole after 20 years. Although the Parole Reform Act made things worse in some ways, now we finally had a lever – something to work with. Prior to that we'd had nothing but hope.

But again the Northern Territory Government had other ideas. They decided to apply to extend Heiss's non-parole period too, probably because of the escapes.

'I got right to the very end – four months off finishing 20 years – and then they decided to try to give me another five years. It was like being tried all over again. It was a very tough blow', says Heiss wryly.

Carolyn still didn't give up hope, although she admits that she might have 'dropped her bundle' behind closed doors. 'I never let on to Daniel though. I couldn't lay that on him as well; he depended on me to be strong.'

'Throughout it all, Carolyn was my wise counsellor', says Heiss. 'Towards the end of the sentence, they'd let me ring her up whenever I wanted – every hour – so I used to discharge all the negative energy by talking to Carolyn. Just trying to stay sane was always difficult inside, but that time was particularly tough.'

The application to extend Heiss's non-parole period was heard on the 22 June 2009, and the judgement was made in Heiss's favour:

I am satisfied that over the last 14 years, Heiss has rehabilitated himself to a stage where he is ready to be released back into the community once he has completed his reintegration. I am satisfied that he has good prospects of further rehabilitation once released back into the community by virtue of his ongoing family support, his relationship with Ms Wilkinson and his community support group.

Together with statements from supporters including a couple of journalists, a federal policeman and his psychologist, among many others, Carolyn's strength, determination and steadfast loyalty had obviously impressed the judge.

The affidavit of Ms Wilkinson indicates that she has been in close contact with Heiss since January 1996. She has made frequent visits to Heiss since then. When Heiss was held at the Alice Springs prison, she still managed to attend on a regular basis. She was only able to speak to him on the telephone for 10 minutes once a month whilst he was in Alice Springs. During the period of seven years whilst he was in the Alice Springs prison she says 'we wrote over 3,000 letters to each other'. Since his transfer back to Berrimah prison, she says that she was able to visit him twice a week for one hour and from October 2004 telephone access was daily.

She confirms also that he is keen to use his artistic skills to become a graphic designer and that he is keen to work. She states that she is convinced that Heiss would do nothing to jeopardise his freedom when released back into the community and that she has no hesitation in having him reside with her and in continuing their relationship.

Heiss didn't have to serve another five years. 'Deep down, I always felt confident that I would win that one. They had no grounds to extend my sentence.' But it was too soon to break out the champagne – or water in Heiss's case. He still needed to be cleared for parole by the Parole Board.

But first Carolyn and Heiss had the bizarre experience of watching the actual murderer being released ahead of Heiss. For a few moments, Carolyn had even thought it was a joke, given that Peter Kamm's release was announced on April Fools' Day. Carolyn was incensed.

I actually rang up ABC radio and asked is this for real or a joke? And they said that it wasn't a joke. Well, it should have been. You honestly couldn't make this stuff up. The murderer gets released ahead of his accomplice? It was completely bewildering. I mean, what the fuck? Daniel was an accessory, sure, but the shooter got out first!

The last hurdle the pair had to face was parole for Heiss. His application failed seven times, but on 1 July 2011, Territory Day, it was publically announced that he had at last been successful.

Reaching The Unreachable Star

Daniel Heiss had been in prison for 22 years, and in a relationship with Carolyn for the last 17 of them. His release led to a lot of firsts for them . . . their first proper date, meal together, time alone. At home together at last, it was also the first time that they had been able to talk – properly talk – without anyone listening in.

In there, you have to always be careful and keep your mind straight. Big Brother was always watching and listening – and they were always on my case given that I'd escaped twice. You can never relax, or fully express yourself. Often, they'll take issue with little things and say, 'Well, you said this on the phone. . .' and then I'd get in trouble.

Other firsts were things that seem mundane to anyone who has been living in the community for the past 22 years. 'He had to learn everything', says Carolyn.

> ATMs weren't really around when he went in. Mobile phones, the internet – everything is more complicated today than it ever was and he really had no idea how difficult the 21st century had become. His mum would ask him to email her, and he'd say: 'Well, I don't really do emails'. He was used to writing letters and talking on the phone.

'I wasn't nervous about how we'd go on the outside', says Heiss. 'I'd been to her place in my mind's eye, and because I was so comfortable with her, I was also comfortable at her place when I came here the first time. I always felt like it was my home too.'

Heiss had a long wish list of things he'd dreamed about doing with Carolyn when he got out. 'To eat a fish dinner together, to go swimming together, basically everything was new to me. I wasn't allowed to have a drink though, because of the alcohol restrictions with my parole. I just wanted to be like any other couple.'

As fun as some of these things undoubtedly were, adjusting to life on the outside was still a big challenge for Heiss. 'Without support, it's easy to fall flat on your face but I had really good, strong support all around me. I had Carolyn.'

Carolyn's support on the outside was to prove just as crucial as it had been during those long years in prison, but it hasn't been easy for her either.

He was very edgy at first – understandably, given the environment he'd been living in for so many years. When he first got out, we worked out a phrase that he could say to me whenever he was feeling uncomfortable somewhere and we needed to leave. We set up many little escape routes like that for whenever he might be feeling anxious or unhappy.

Any methods they used to keep Heiss feeling secure had been developed on their own initiative. 'Support after his release? You've got to be kidding! They don't do that up here. I asked Corrections to send me information on the effects of long-term incarceration, but all they gave me was stuff I had already found on the internet.'

Carolyn considers it very short-sighted to simply open the door and send long-term prisoners on their way. 'Lack of support is why, I think, some people re-offend. They find it too hard on the outside, and they're naturally drawn back to what is familiar and somewhat safe – somewhere they know.'

Today, Carolyn and Heiss live quietly in northern Australia, well under the radar and away from would-be curious eyes. She's been busy working on the book of his experiences, and has more planned – *The Hard Yards* covering the years he spent in Alice Springs, and

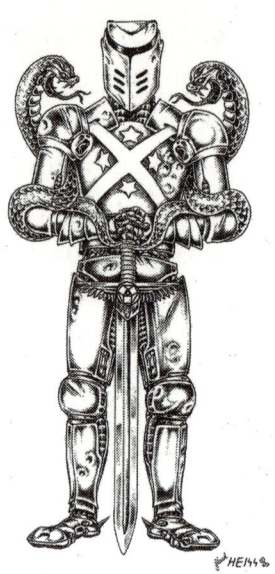

This Bird is Flown, about the lead-up to his eventual release. While she included many of the letters they wrote during the first year of their relationship in *Blood on the Wire*, there are still another 4200 or more from which she can draw material.

Heiss is happy to be leading a simple life. He's not inspired to paint at the moment – too many memories of prison, perhaps – but thinks he will get back to it one day soon. He's content doing short stints of paid work, leaving him time to dabble with pottery and ceramics, noodle around on his guitar, and simply explore and re-adapt to the world he was removed from for so many years.

He is coming up to the second anniversary of his release, and both Carolyn and he are relieved that the years of constant battle are now behind them. It was only at the end of the long, long process that a friend posted the song 'The Impossible Dream' onto Carolyn's website, saying that this song could have been written for her. Carolyn credits love and laughter – the very best medicine of all – for the fact that they have finally achieved their own impossible dream.